Tracking DOCTOR LONECLOUD
Showman to Legend Keeper

by RUTH HOLMES WHITEHEAD
including the memoir of JERRY LONECLOUD,
reconstructed and annotated by Ruth Holmes Whitehead
from interview notes by Clara Dennis

GOOSE LANE EDITIONS *and* NOVA SCOTIA MUSEUM

Edited by Roberta Lee.
Cover photos: Jerry Lonecloud, 1880s: NSARM, Halifax, N-6151;
Jerry Lonecloud, 1920: NSM History Collection, N-5010.
Cover and interior design by Julie Scriver.
Printed in Canada by AGMV Marquis.
10 9 8 7 6 5 4 3 2 1

Most of the photographs in this book are from the History Collection of the Nova Scotia Museum, Halifax (NSM) and from the Nova Scotia Archives and Records Management, Halifax (NSARM). These and other photographs are reprinted with the permission of the copyright holders.

WARNING: Jerry Lonecloud describes many remedies and tonics made from plant and animal parts. Please *do not* experiment with these. Some are highly toxic and can cause death. For treatment of illness, consult your physician.

National Library of Canada Cataloguing in Publication

Whitehead, Ruth Holmes
Tracking Doctor Lonecloud: showman to legend keeper / by Ruth Holmes Whitehead; including the memoir of Jerry Lonecloud reconstructed and annotated by Ruth Holmes Whitehead from interview notes by Clara Dennis.

Co-published by: Nova Scotia Museum.
Includes bibliographical references and index.
ISBN 0-86492-356-2

1. Lonecloud, Jerry, 1854-1930. 2. Micmac Indians — Nova Scotia — Biography. 3. Entertainers — Nova Scotia — Biography. I. Lonecloud, Jerry, 1854-1930. II. Dennis, Clara, 1881-1954. III. Nova Scotia Museum IV. Title.

E99.M6W474 2002   971.6'004973   C2002-903836-7

Published with the financial support of the Canada Council for the Arts, the Government of Canada through the Book Publishing Industry Development Program, and the New Brunswick Culture and Sports Secretariat.

Goose Lane Editions
469 King Street
Fredericton, New Brunswick
CANADA E3B 1E5
www.gooselane.com

Nova Scotia Museum
1747 Summer Street
Halifax, Nova Scotia
CANADA B3H 3A6
www.museum.gov.ns.ca

For Trudy Sable, who, most of all, made it happen.

JERRY LONECLOUD AND
THE NOVA SCOTIA MUSEUM

Over a period of twenty years, Jerry Lonecloud
collected artifacts and specimens for the
Provincial Museum of Nova Scotia,
now the Nova Scotia Museum, at
1747 Summer Street, Halifax, NS.

During the long friendship and collaboration
of Lonecloud and Harry Piers, the museum's
curator, Piers recorded oral histories and
stories, Mi'kmaw vocabulary, place-names,
and observations on the habits of animals,
just as Lonecloud recounted them in his visits
to the museum. This information is archived
with the Piers Papers in the Nova Scotia
Museum Library and can be viewed at
http://museum.gov.ns.ca/resources

CONTENTS

PREFACE
The Tracking of Doctor Lonecloud

THE STORY YOU ARE about to read is one of a well-known and colourful Mi'kmaw man, Doctor Jerry Lonecloud, who travelled extensively throughout North America. During Doctor Lonecloud's travels, he gained a great amount of personal knowledge of different cultures, and in return he shared his vast knowledge of the Mi'kmaw people.

The information collected by the late Clara Dennis and the late Harry Piers and assembled by Ruth Holmes Whitehead into this book is only a small picture of what is known of Doctor Lonecloud and his adventures. The story of his many trips from early childhood to when he left this world to join our ancestors is very intriguing. In my many years of research at the Nova Scotia Archives and the National Archives of Canada, I have found his name on hundreds of government documents.

As the story unfolds, Germain (Jerry) Bartlett Alexis, son of Abram Alexis and Mary Ann Tomah, both Nova Scotia Mi'kmaq, was born in Belfast, Maine, on the Fourth of July, 1854. Jerry spent a lot of time with his father and uncle, and at an early age he was taught recognition and understanding of the Mi'kmaw way of life. His knowledge of herbal plants and the creation of medicinal remedies began when he was a child. He was also well known for his guiding and sporting activities, which he learned from his mother's relatives, who were well known as guides and sportsmen in the nineteenth century.

Jerry's parents died in the United States when he was about fourteen years of age, leaving him to care for himself, his two younger brothers, and a sister. Jerry took responsibility very well and travelled for several years, experiencing many adventures with his siblings. Jerry managed to bring his family safely home to Nova Scotia about 1869. Shortly after, however, his brothers passed away, but he was there for his sister until she was married.

During his visits, Jerry met and talked with many other Mi'kmaw people, and he retained a lot of knowledge from the stories he was told. Later in life, he retold these stories, and many are recorded in the legends in this book. We can only imagine the number of untold stories and adventures and the many people he got to know.

Jerry went back to the United States around 1879 or 1880. As we track Jerry after his return to the States, we find he joined Healy and Bigelow's Wild West Show. This is where he received his name of Doctor Lonecloud, given to him by another culture to sell "Indian" authenticity to the white audiences. After many adventures on the Wild West Show circuit, he finally returned to New Brunswick, where he met his wife-to-be, Elizabeth Paul, a young Maliseet woman. The story and the adventures then carry on, with Doctor Jerry Lonecloud having his own show that travelled across the Atlantic area.

Around 1892, he settled down in the Liscomb Mills area of Nova Scotia. Here he made a living for a number of years selling herbal medicines and crafts and guiding. His wife Elizabeth was well known for her work and was also a midwife. Throughout his years in the Liscomb area, Jerry Lonecloud and his family produced many medicine shows and sold herbal remedies that were good for either man or beast. When Doctor Lonecloud and his family later moved to Tufts Cove, Dartmouth, he continued his production of herbal remedies and his travels down through the Eastern Shore, where every spring people anxiously awaited his arrival with his remedies.

Jerry Lonecloud became involved in Mi'kmaw politics and was elected Second Sub-Chief for Halifax County. At this time, he became involved with the federal Department of Indian Affairs in the care of Halifax County Indians and their lands. With the assistance of his friend Harry Piers, he began questioning the Department of Indian Affairs about their creation of Indian reserves in the area. He questioned why the Department did not establish an Indian reserve at Tufts Cove. When he realized that Mi'kmaq were only squatting there, Jerry questioned the Department of Indian Affairs again, saying that if the Department weren't willing to purchase the land, they should assist with relocating the people from Tufts Cove to several other Mi'kmaw areas. Unfortunately, his appeal fell on deaf ears, and he was given several excuses — there was no money available, and there were already too many reserves in Halifax County that were not in use.

On December 6, 1917, while Doctor Lonecloud and his wife Elizabeth were away from their settlement at Tufts Cove, tragedy occurred in Halifax Harbour. The Halifax Explosion destroyed parts of Halifax and Dartmouth, with a large number of people killed and injured. The explosion caused personal tragedy for the Lonecloud family. Not only were many of their friends and relatives killed and the small Mi'kmaw settlement at Tufts Cove destroyed, but Jerry and Elizabeth lost two daughters, Rosie and Hannah. With even more vigour, Jerry Lonecloud wrote letters to the Department of Indian Affairs wanting resettlement of the survivors to either Indian Brook, Ship Harbour, Elmsdale, Enfield, or the new reserve in Truro.

Around 1930, after Doctor Lonecloud's death, his wife Elizabeth moved with her daughter Libby to the Millbrook Reserve in Truro, where she lived until her death in 1961. Elizabeth's last request was to be buried beside her son Louis at the Sacred Heart Cemetery on the Millbrook Reserve.

This is where the story ends, with memories and tales from our elders in several communities remembering Doctor Jerry Lonecloud and his family.

Donald M. Julien
Millbrook First Nation
2001

Jerry Lonecloud in 1920, photographed by Climo Studios, Halifax, for the Nova Scotia Museum. (NSM, N-5010)

INTRODUCTION

JERRY LONECLOUD, THE CENTRAL FIGURE in this book, was a Mi'kmaw medicine man, hunter, and storyteller. He was probably born on July 4, 1854, in Belfast, Maine, to Mi'kmaw parents from Nova Scotia, and he died in Halifax, Nova Scotia, on April 16, 1930. From 1923 through 1929, Halifax reporter Clara Dennis interviewed Lonecloud on a number of occasions and recorded his words in field notebooks. During the course of these interviews, Lonecloud told Dennis the story of his life up until about 1890, the time of his marriage. He also provided a wealth of information about Mi'kmaw history, folk medicine, ceremonies, language, and legends, as well as plants, animals, and geography. The core of *Tracking Doctor Lonecloud: Showman to Legend Keeper* is an edited version of Dennis's notes from the Lonecloud interviews, the earliest known Mi'kmaw autobiography and memoir.

I first became aware of Jerry Lonecloud in 1972, as I began working with the collections and records at the Nova Scotia Museum. Harry Piers, curator of the Provincial Museum of Nova Scotia (now called the Nova Scotia Museum) from 1899 until 1940, had been Lonecloud's friend. In August 1910, Lonecloud began bringing artifacts to Piers at the museum, and the two men established a relationship of mutual trust and respect that lasted for the next twenty years. On several occasions, Piers arranged for portrait photographs of Lonecloud to be taken by local studios for the museum collection.

Piers (1870-1940), a brilliant man interested in everything, made copious notes on many subjects, ranging from Mi'kmaw culture to topics of natural history, using information which Lonecloud provided. Piers might become intrigued by gypsum, for example, or wild rhododendrons. Lonecloud would tell him where to find them and bring in samples. Lonecloud

Harry Piers, Curator of the Provincial Museum, in 1933. (NSM, N-9620)

became Piers's primary advisor on Mi'kmaw matters, and in a way Piers returned the favour: while Lonecloud could read and write, Piers sometimes drafted more formal letters for him, including a number of petitions to the Department of Indian Affairs. Other scholars began writing to Piers, asking him for Lonecloud's help with their research. Piers's documents and correspondence would eventually shed light for me on matters Lonecloud discussed with Clara Dennis.

Harry Piers died suddenly in January 1940, and most of the museum's Mi'kmaw collection was placed in storage. After 1970, these documents, photographs, notes, and artifacts were moved to the new Nova Scotia Museum building on Summer Street in Halifax. There were boxes and boxes of artifacts, and I was cataloguing them. Brian Preston, History

Curator at the museum, had begun typing up some of Piers's notes, and this material caught my interest because it taught me more about the things I was examining. By a curious twist of fate, the Nova Scotia Museum in 1973 received a collection of black-and-white photographs of Mi'kmaw people taken by Clara Dennis before World War II. I was cataloguing them as well. By comparing them with the portraits of Lonecloud commissioned by Piers, I was able to show that two of Dennis's photos were of Jerry Lonecloud. There my encounter with Lonecloud rested, except that I used quite a bit of Piers's Lonecloud material in a 1991 book of excerpted documents dealing with the Mi'kmaw people, *The Old Man Told Us.*

Although Peter Morris of the Nova Scotia Museum had told me that there were Dennis papers in the Nova Scotia Archives, I didn't suspect that they contained information about Lonecloud or the Mi'kmaq. Then Trudy Sable, with whom I had collaborated on a number of research projects, learned about the amount of Mi'kmaw content in the Dennis papers from Marilyn Moore, a Saint Mary's University graduate student who was conducting research on Clara Dennis.

Finally, in 1992, Trudy Sable dragged me off to the Nova Scotia Archives to see what really *was* there. I remember our stunned amazement as we began decoding Dennis's handwriting to find the enormous amount of information about the Mi'kmaq, most of it in Jerry Lonecloud's own words (Dennis had also interviewed other Mi'kmaq), and much of it recorded nowhere else.

Clarissa Archibald Dennis (1881-1954) was a reporter for the *Halifax Herald,* a local newspaper owned by her father, Senator William Dennis. She may have met Lonecloud when she was covering the 1923 *Hector* celebration, commemorating the one hundred and fiftieth anniversary of the landing of the Scottish settlers at Pictou, Nova Scotia. Lonecloud was an important player in that re-enactment, and many photographs of him were taken at that time. Her two photographs of Lonecloud, we found, were taken outside her home at 45 Coburg Road, Halifax, probably at the time of her first interview with him.

Clara Dennis recorded her sessions with Lonecloud in pencil in children's scribblers, sometimes taking notes, sometimes putting down Lonecloud's exact words. She wrote rapidly to keep up with him, occasionally using

Clara Dennis, the travel writer and reporter who interviewed Jerry Lonecloud, 1931. (NSARM, Clara Dennis Collection, 1981-541, Item 1151)

shorthand notation for short words such as *the, and,* or *that.* Apparently she used to read back to him, at subsequent interviews, stories he had previously told her. In one notebook, she wrote that he approved her spelling of a Mi'kmaw word, and in another, she recorded that he responded, "You put too much white people's ideas." After Lonecloud's death, Dennis authored three travel books about Nova Scotia: *Down in Nova Scotia* (1934), *More About Nova Scotia* (1937), and *Cape Breton Over* (1942). Although she never mentions Lonecloud by name, some data from the interviews appears in these works; she simply refers to him as "the old Indian." Dennis's field notebooks, which include twenty-three dated interviews and other undated conversations, were discovered in an Atlantic Trust vault in 1989 and given to the Nova Scotia Archives and Records Management, Halifax.

Trudy Sable and I spent months transcribing the Dennis notebooks, word for word and line for line, exactly as written. The difficulty of deciphering her handwriting can be appreciated by looking at photos of pages from the original scribblers (see pages 18-19). A copy of our original transcript has been presented to the Nova Scotia Archives and placed with the Dennis papers. It includes some editorial comment from me, as well as some corrections of Dennis's phonetic spellings of the Mi'kmaw language made by linguist Bernie Francis.

After we had completed the transcription, I spent the next few years editing and reworking it and compiling the Piers material on Jerry Lonecloud for the purpose of clarifying some of the things Lonecloud told Clara Dennis. Trudy Sable used some of the material from the transcripts in her 1996 Masters Thesis for Saint Mary's University, "Another Look in the Mirror: Research Into the Foundation for Developing an Alternative Science Curriculum for Mi'kmaw Children."

Over the following years, Trudy and I actually tracked Lonecloud through the landscape, I photographing and she videotaping places mentioned in his interviews with Dennis. While we were filming in Little Liscomb, Guysborough County, Walter Baker came down from his house nearby and talked to us about his grandfather's experiences with Lonecloud. Trudy and I also canoed up Lake Charlotte in Halifax County, looking for sites. We clambered over rocks in the Musquodoboit River, and I remember wading, fully dressed, up to my waist in Shubenacadie Grand Lake, trying to find a rock formation Lonecloud had said was important to the Mi'kmaq. All in all, backtrailing this remarkable person has been a real adventure.

In recent years, I have encountered people who thought Lonecloud was not a "real Indian" at all, much less a Mi'kmaw man. This suspicion is false. He was born Mi'kmaq, raised Mi'kmaq, spoke Mi'kmaq, lived and died a Mi'kmaq. His memoirs dictated to Dennis, his conversations with Piers, and my own genealogical research prove that beyond doubt. Following in his footsteps, through documents, photos, and through the land he knew so well, I have come to have a great respect for him. I'd like to express my gratitude to him and my vast appreciation for the information he preserved for all of us.

Ruth Holmes Whitehead
1992-2002

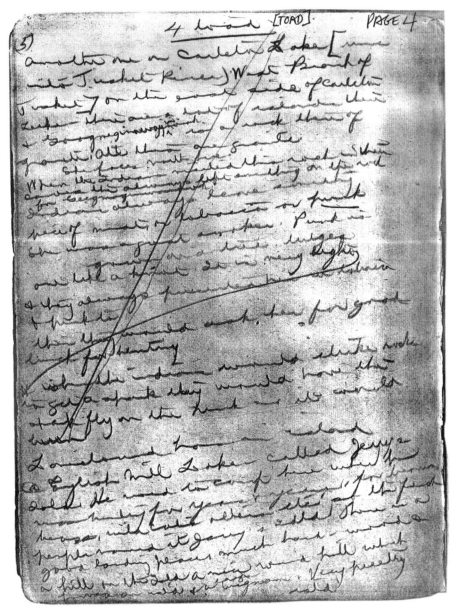

Two pages from a scribbler in which Clara Dennis recorded Jerry Lonecloud's conversations with her. (NSARM, MG1 Vol. 2867 #1, pp. 4-5)

Jerry Lonecloud, photographed at the Gauvin and Gentzel Studio,
Halifax, 2 February 1929, for the Provincial Museum of Nova Scotia.
(NSM, N-12,714)

ACKNOWLEDGEMENTS

I WOULD LIKE TO THANK the many people who helped in the quest to find Lonecloud. My greatest debt is to Trudy Sable, now an intercultural researcher and consultant and Director of the Labrador Project, Gorsebrook Research Institute, Saint Mary's University. Ralph Muise of the Nova Scotia Department of Lands and Forests took Bernie Francis and Trudy Sable by canoe up the Tusket River. Later, Bob Bancroft took Trudy and me to the Liscomb River area; archaeologists Rob Ferguson, Ron Nash, and Scott Buchanan came along and provided a canoe to explore rock formations in Little Liscomb harbour. Ron Nash showed me, in a pouring rain, the place on the St. Mary's River where, according to Lonecloud, the Abbé Maillard had established a mission in the early 1700s. Blake Conrad shared some genealogical data. Joe Nickell sent the article on John Wilkes Booth.

In September 1996, Cicely Berglund drove me down to Grand Isle, Vermont, in Lake Champlain, where Lonecloud spent some of his boyhood, and on to Waterbury, Vermont, where his mother is buried. On another occasion, Carmelita Robertson took me to Lower Ohio on the Roseway River, Nova Scotia, where Lonecloud's father was born. Deborah Trask of the Nova Scotia Museum drove me to Windsor, Nova Scotia, where we searched the Old Burying Ground in vain for the memorial to Thomas Phillips, Lonecloud's maternal grandfather.

In 1997, my daughter Sarah Whitehead drove me once again to Guysborough County, where I acquired invaluable information about Lonecloud's years there from Ruth Legge of Liscomb Mills. Her forebears, the Rumleys, had befriended Lonecloud and his family when they settled in the community. Legge asked her relatives Kenneth Rumley and Katie Rumley about their memories of Lonecloud. She also interviewed Grace Rodenizer, who

The Roseway River, Shelburne County, near the village of Ohio, where Jerry Lonecloud's father was born. (Ruth Holmes Whitehead, 1996)

had lived near the Lonecloud household when she was a child and who could remember stories about him and his children. During my visit, Ruth Legge took me to the site of Lonecloud's cabin near Liscomb Lodge and pointed out the foundation stones, now completely overgrown by trees. She also granted me an interview and afterwards painstakingly corrected my rough draft of her transcribed words.

I am grateful to all the people who have helped me with the illustrations for this work. Scott Robson of the Nova Scotia Museum found several Lonecloud photos for me and critiqued text and captions. Harald Prins at Kansas State University sent me an article with a photo of a medicine bottle label showing "Dr. Lone Cloud." Joe Nickell of the Center for Scientific Inquiry owns a Kickapoo bottle and a Morse's Indian Root Pills chromolithograph; he arranged for Tom Flynn to make digital photographs of them at no charge. Bruce Bourque of the Maine State Museum purchased a print of a Lonecloud photo for me, and Charlie Dillman of Middle Musquodoboit helped me find Danny Johnson, the owner of the original glass negative of this shot. Johnson sold it to the Nova Scotia Museum just in time for inclusion in this book and also allowed us to copy other glass negatives in his collection. Steve Powell of the Nova Scotia Museum did digital photography at a moment's notice. Ron Merrick, Roger Lloyd, and Richard Plander of the Nova Scotia Department of Education's Learning Resources and Technology Division developed and printed photographs for this project and skillfully copied the old Lonecloud portraits in the History Collection of the Nova Scotia Museum.

My thanks to the Nova Scotia Archives and Records Management Staff, in particular to Garry Shutlak, Margaret Campbell, and Lois Yorke, for ten years of help while I was working on the Dennis material housed at the Archives and for several photographs from their collections. Heartfelt thanks are also due to Alex Wilson and Marian Munro, Nova Scotia Museum botanists, who helped identify many of the plants mentioned by Lonecloud and provided the Latin names for most of them.

My deepest appreciation and admiration go to linguist Bernie Francis for his work on this manuscript. He has ensured that the spellings of all recoverable Mi'kmaw words are correct and that the meanings are accurate. He also indicated a few places where he was unable to figure out just what Lonecloud or Dennis meant. Bernie Francis, Alan Knockwood, and Donald Julien were our outside readers for the manuscript.

Finally, I am profoundly grateful to Mrs. Marion Christie, who, as Clara Dennis's closest surviving relative, gave her consent for Miss Dennis's notes of her interviews with Jerry Lonecloud to be used in this publication. Without her generosity, Lonecloud's information would still be buried in obscurity.

R.H.W.

A NOTE ABOUT SPELLING

READERS WILL NOTICE three ways of spelling the tribal identifier and language: *Mi'kmaw*, *Mi'kmaq* and *Micmac*. *Mi'kmaq* (the plural form) or *Mi'kmaw* (the singular form) is the preferred spelling today. Prior to the development of the Francis-Smith orthography for writing in this language, there were many variations in the way the word was spelled by English and French writers. Some even split it, making it Mic Mac. Others, ignorant of the fact that this is the plural form, added a final *s*. Harry Piers and Clara Dennis both wrote "Micmac" or "Micmacs." I have left their spellings as they wrote them, but I have used "Mi'kmaq" or "Mi'kmaw," as appropriate, in my own writing.

Because there is some confusion, to say the least, about when to use the plural form in English and when to use the singular, I consulted with Bernie Francis, one of the developers of the Francis-Smith orthography, himself a Mi'kmaw as well as a linguist. Here is what he says:

> The tribal name, when used as a noun in English, takes the plural form, Mi'kmaq. One writes and says, "They are Mi'kmaq." This is always the case, except when one is speaking of a single person. In that case, the singular form, Mi'kmaw, is used. "She is a Mi'kmaw." The language is also called Mi'kmaq when used as a noun: "He speaks fluent Mi'kmaq."

> This all changes when the word is used as an adjective. The Mi'kmaw First Nations people now prefer that we all get used to seeing and using the singular form, Mi'kmaw, as the adjectival form in English, even when the adjective is modifying a plural noun. So, according to Bernie Francis, one would say, "They are Mi'kmaw people." "He speaks the Mi'kmaw language." "Those are Mi'kmaw beadwork suspenders."

One of the last portraits of Jerry Lonecloud, taken on 2 February 1929 at the Gauvin and Gentzel Studio, Halifax, for the Provincial Museum of Nova Scotia. (NSM, N-12,715)

ONE
The Life of Jerry Lonecloud

WHO WAS JERRY LONECLOUD? Born into a Mi'kmaw family, he was called by several names during the course of his life: Haselmah Laksi, Germain Bartlett Alexis, Jerry Luxcey, Jeremiah Bartlett, Doctor Lonecloud. In his later years, he billed himself as "medicine man to the Micmac nation." An enigmatic figure, he served not only as an advocate for Mi'kmaw Nova Scotians but also as an eloquent interpreter of native culture. Perhaps Lonecloud's own words provide a good starting point in the search for who he was: "I was a showman!" Indeed, he spent half his life touring with medicine shows, one of them his own.

According to historian Arrell Gibson, "in early America, itinerant drug peddlers found sales slow. . . . Thus, to push their products, American medicine men revived the medieval practice of providing entertainment to attract crowds." After the Civil War, these medicine shows became increasingly popular, and by 1900, they "numbered in the hundreds." The biggest of them all was the Kickapoo Indian Medicine Company. Also known as Healey and Bigelow's Wild West Show, it was the brainchild of two promoters, "Texas Charlie" Bigelow and Colonel John Healey. Bigelow and Healey made deals with Indian agents for native performers by "pledging protection and good care, and thirty dollars a month and keep for each Indian." Gibson's article, "Medicine Show," in *The American West: Magazine of the Western History Association*, is accompanied by an illustration, "Photographs of Some of the Famous Medicine Men Engaged at the Wigwam." The caption reveals how Healey and Bigelow represented their native performers: each medicine man is given the title "Doctor" and provided with a "typical" Indian name, such as Dr. Poor Fox, Dr. Floating Poplar, Dr. Big Moon, and Dr. Clear Water, as well as Dr. Lonecloud. In the print, Lonecloud's face floats, unrecognizable, right above the line promoting "Kickapoo Indian Oil — A Quick Cure for all Pains, External and Internal."[1]

Lonecloud's memoirs are sprinkled with white men's phrases such as "happy hunting grounds," "tom-toms," and "squaws." He had obviously learned to communicate in English in phrases which the other culture had propagated and with which it was familiar, thereby presenting himself as a kind of icon or caricature of Indian-ness. He was indeed a showman, and the ability to communicate with one's audience in a language they understand is a showman's greatest asset.

Jerry definitely traded on his native ancestry, even down to the name by which he was known for the rest of his life — Lonecloud. He evidently told Nova Scotian folklorist Helen Creighton that his name came from a "lone cloud" which appeared in the sky when he was born and his parents were considering a name.[2] One of the great ironies of his life is that this "Indian" name was actually given him by another culture to sell "Indian" authenticity to non-native audiences.

Clearly Jerry Lonecloud was a man with a foot in two very different worlds. In his Mi'kmaw world, he seems to have been christened Germain. He often told Harry Piers that his "Micmac name" was "Haselmah." Selmah (now written Slme'n in Mi'kmaw orthography) was the way a Mi'kmaw would say the French name Germain, with the s replacing the soft g, and the l replacing the r sound. Jerry was short for Germain, and when he spoke English, many people, including Piers, assumed it was short for Jeremiah and believed that Haselmah was another name entirely. Père Pacifique, a Capuchin priest working with the Mi'kmaq and author of a work on Mi'kmaw place names in Canada, inadvertently clarified this mystery about "Haselmah" while writing about one of Jerry's ancestors, after whom a lake had been named: "Tomaeg . . . called after Thomas Germain (Selmah), great-grandfather of Lone Cloud (Alexis Selmah)."[3] As to the "Ha" part of his name, Lonecloud pronounced certain Mi'kmaw words with an initial h or ha sound that may reflect a variant he heard as a child (there is no h in modern Mi'kmaq).

There is also some confusion surrounding Lonecloud's use of two surnames. The first, Alexis, written Laksi in Mi'kmaq, has variously been spelled "Lexey," "Luxcey," and "Luzzie" by the English. Lonecloud informed

Stephen Bartlett Laksi, Jerry Lonecloud's uncle, who was born at Salmon River, Yarmouth County, in 1819 and died about 1902. He was Chief of the Gravel Pit Reserve, outside Yarmouth. (NSM, 17.46 (4578), glass negative)

Piers that the family normally used the surname Laksi when in Shelburne County, where they had Laksi relatives, but that they went by Bartlett in Yarmouth County. He also once said they used Bartlett in his younger days, perhaps during the family's time in the United States. On the other hand, Clara Dennis recorded him as saying, "We was Luxceys," when speaking of his childhood.

The Alexis family name probably originated with a man baptized Alexis (Laksi) and whose children took their father's given name as their surname. Lonecloud's paternal grandfather, Etienne Bartlett Alexis, was a Mi'kmaw who married an Acadian woman. His name is written Ekien Laksi, according to the modern Francis-Smith orthography for the Mi'kmaw language. He was more often known by his nickname, Ekien Wisow.

His younger son, Lonecloud's father, was named Abram or Abraham and nicknamed Musi Wisow. The older son, Lonecloud's uncle, was born in 1819; he was named Stephen (Etienne) and called Ekien Wisow like his father. During Lonecloud's lifetime, his Uncle Stephen was Chief of the Gravel Pit Reserve, two miles out of Yarmouth, Nova Scotia, on the Yarmouth-Tusket Road. He died in 1902, aged about eighty-three.[4] In his conversations with Clara Dennis, Lonecloud recalled that his father and uncle received instruction in Latin from Abbé Sigogne and that they sang in the chapel choir at Eel Brook, near Tusket. He also noted that his grand-

Steven Laksi, Jerry Lonecloud's first cousin, at the Gravel Pit Reserve, Yarmouth County, about 1930. Clara Dennis took the photograph and interviewed him briefly. (NSM, N-14,767)

father and father were both healers and that his father and uncle took him in the woods and taught him how to recognize and gather medicinal herbs.[5]

Lonecloud's mother, Mary Ann, was the only daughter of a noted guide, Tom Phillips. She took her father's French baptismal name, Thomas (Jerry pronounced it Tomah), as her surname, in accordance with a widely used eighteenth- and nineteenth-century custom. Tom Phillips was the son of a Mi'kmaw father and an Acadian mother. He was born at Big Indian Lake, near Indian Hill at the head of St. Margaret's Bay, Halifax County. In later life he lived at St. Croix, Hants County, where he had a "sort of half-way house" and acted as a guide for military officers who wished to hunt moose.

One of these sportsmen, Campbell Hardy, described his first meeting with Tom Phillips: "I arrived [September 1853] at a bridge over the St. Croix River. . . . Here lived the Indians of whom I was in search, not in camps, but in small neat log houses, situated in a cultivated patch cleared by them. The owner of one of the huts, an old Indian hunter as my driver informed me, was engaged in hoeing a patch of potatoes when we arrived. He acknowledged my verbose salutation by a slight inclination of the head . . . sat down on a rock, and lighting his pipe, told me I might say what I wanted. The Indians are generally noted for the paucity of their words, but this old fellow was the most taciturn I ever met with." Later, Phillips's neighbours recommended him to Hardy as "one of the smartest Indians in the province and . . . a good hunter." When Hardy set off on a hunting trip with Tom Phillips, he observed that Phillips "had a tight little canoe, one of the prettiest models and best goers I ever saw."[6]

On July 4, probably in 1854, a son was born to Mary Ann Tomah and Abram Bartlett Alexis, then living in Belfast, Maine: their oldest surviving child, Germain Bartlett Alexis. When Jerry was a small child, he and his family traveled extensively along the St. Lawrence River and the Great Lakes, hunting and gathering herbs. His parents sold medicines and tonics, possibly Morse's Indian Root Pills; perhaps they were part of an early medicine show. When he was about six or seven years old, he visited Niagara Falls with his family; they also went by cattle boat down the Erie Canal to New York City. They lived for a time at Kahnawake, in Quebec. When he was about twelve years old, his father took him hunting at the foot of Mount Mansfield in Vermont with some Kahnawake Iroquois. He told Piers that "these Indians hunted and killed red deer and muskrats with a fir bow about five feet long, with hardwood arrows tipped with iron." The bow was "strung with caribou rawhide."[7] In the nineteenth century, guns were a common possession; evidently Jerry's father and his friends enjoyed the challenge of hunting with a bow.

At the start of the Civil War in 1860, Jerry and his family were living on Grand Isle in Lake Champlain, which runs north-south as the border between New York and Vermont. Jerry's father, Abram, enlisted in the Union army with a New York battalion out of Plattsburg and served for three years. He then re-enlisted as a paid substitute for a neighbour in North Hero, Grand Isle, who was drafted and did not wish to serve. While he was away, his wife and children lived on the payment from this neighbour, five hundred dollars in gold.

After the war, tragedy struck the family. On 24 April 1865, Jerry's father was selected, along with twenty-five other soldiers of the Sixteenth New York Cavalry, to track and capture John Wilkes Booth, Abraham Lincoln's assassin. A reward of $100,000 had been offered for catching Booth. In his memoirs, Lonecloud relates Abram's account of Booth's capture. With Booth taken into custody and dead, Abram returned to his wife and family, who had moved to Waterbury, Vermont, during his absence. After a short visit, he left for New York City to obtain his share of the reward: $1,653.85.[8]

Tom Phillips, Mary Ann's father, had died in 1864. She told her children that he had left her a piece of land at the head of St. Margaret's Bay, near the place he was born, and that they were going home to Nova Scotia as soon as Abram came back with the money. But his wife and children never saw him again. They finally concluded that he had been murdered for his share of the reward. Mary Ann died a short time afterwards, late in the spring of 1865, and was buried in Waterbury, Vermont, on the Onion River. She left behind four orphaned children: Jerry, two younger boys, and a girl, Sarah.

Young Jerry, now the head of the family, decided to follow his parents' plan of returning to Nova Scotia. His mother had left some money. He set out with his brothers and sister on a two-year odyssey that involved travel by train, steamship, sailboat and canoe, camping along the way. Finally, with the help of some of their mother's Nova Scotian relatives, they came home across the Bay of Fundy from New Brunswick. The exact fate of the two younger brothers and Sarah after their arrival is unclear. Jerry's two brothers did not live to grow up, but Sarah survived, married a man with the surname Michael, and apparently was widowed but still alive in 1911 at Bear River.[9]

Jerry lived for a time in southwestern Nova Scotia with an elderly man, likely a relative, named Peter Charles, or Saln (Mi'kmaq for Charles). They hunted and trapped on the lakes feeding into the Tusket River, and when Saln died, Jerry brought his body to the Eel Brook Chapel for burial. Later he lived in Bear River with one of his father's Alexis relatives, Chief James Meuse.

Jerry Lonecloud told Harry Piers about various incidents that illustrate his prowess during this period of his life. For example, he was in a canoe off of Digby with two boys and their uncle when the canoe capsized. The man drowned, but Jerry was able to save the lives of the two boys, aged fifteen and thirteen. He received wide acclaim for this courageous act. When he was seventeen or eighteen, he went on a hunting trip as camp boy for well-known Nova Scotia sportsman William Gilpin, along with James Meuse and other native guides. After Gilpin shot a doe caribou at Boundary Lake, he offered Jerry five dollars to carry it eighteen miles to Clark's at Lake Jolly and two dollars more to carry it another eight miles.

Glass medicine bottle, embossed on side. "Healy [sic] and Bigelow." (Collection of Joe Nickell. Photo: Tom Flynn)

Jerry agreed and carried the one-hundred-pound carcass on his back for a total of twenty-six miles.[10]

In the early 1880s, the life of Germain Bartlett Alexis took a dramatic turn. He joined Healey and Bigelow's Wild West Show and returned to the United States, taking the name Lone Cloud, or Lonecloud, as it was later spelled. Eventually he broke away from Healey and Bigelow and formed his own company with at least two other performers, stage-named White Dove and Rolling Thunder; he called his company the Kiowa Medicine Show. When business petered out in Keene, New Hampshire, the company broke up. Lonecloud worked for a while with Buffalo Bill's Wild West show and then went back with Healey and Bigelow. He traveled widely, selling medicines for them as far away as South America, where he contracted malaria. In 1885, he was at Niagara Falls when United States President Ulysses S. Grant died, and he took the train from there to New York to see the funeral on August 8. He finally returned to Canada and began hunting in New Brunswick.

It was in New Brunswick that Lonecloud met his wife-to-be, Elizabeth Paul, a seventeen-year-old Maliseet woman, daughter of Chief Louis Paul of Fredericton; in writing and speech, he called her "Sarbet." With Elizabeth and her brother, Lonecloud traveled around the Maritimes, selling medicines and presenting shows to advertise their products. In one of these productions, Elizabeth played Pocahontas and Lonecloud played Captain John Smith. According to Piers, Lonecloud, who had long hair, "used to have a lotion for strengthening the hair. . . . To illustrate the good effects of his hair lotion, another big Indian would hang onto his hair, but . . . he had a leather strap concealed under the hair, and the man suspended himself from the strap, not the hair!" Elizabeth Paul informed Harry Piers that "the hair tonic which he used to sell about the county was derived

Label of a Healey and Bigleow medicine bottle, "Kickapoo Indian Sagwa." (Collection of Joe Nickell. Photo: Tom Flynn)

from the Ground Hemlock." During one show, when Lonecloud ran out of hair tonic, he filled the bottles with cold tea.[11]

Elizabeth Paul married Jerry Lonecloud in Kentville, Nova Scotia, where they lived on and off for several years. Their first child, Rosie, was born about 1888. Jerry, Elizabeth, and Rosie moved to Liscomb Mills, Guysborough County, around 1892 and lived there for the next eighteen years. They came by sailboat to Liscomb Mills, landing on a little island in the harbour. After they arrived, they were befriended by members of the Rumley family. The Rumleys lent them a log cabin by the dock, where they lived at first, later moving to a simple frame house, where Liscomb Lodge now stands. There they had another seven children, but two of them died young. The six who lived were Rosie, Mary Anne, Jerry, Hannah, Elizabeth (Libby), and Louis Abraham (Lewie), born in 1909 and named for both his grandfathers.[12]

During their Liscomb years, Elizabeth worked in a variety of ways to support the family. According to Ruth Legge, "she used to wash the big white blankets from the Goldenville Mines and did baking and cleaning and anything she could to help make a living." She served as a cook for the mills and as a midwife. Along with her husband, she wove baskets and made beadwork items such as picture frames. Jerry and Elizabeth sold these handicrafts at their medicine shows, which they continued to produce during this period. Ruth Legge reported that Lonecloud "walked every-where, Liscomb Mills to Shubenacadie . . . to Port Bickerton to put on concerts or shows, usually in school houses, primarily to sell his medicines for both man and beast, which he made from plants in the 'old Indian way.'"

Grace Rodenizer, who lived close to the Loneclouds' house in Liscomb when she was a child, played with the Lonecloud children, Hannah, young Jerry, and Libby. She told Ruth Legge what she remembered about Jerry and Elizabeth's lives and personalities.

> [Lonecloud was] a gentleman, kind and gentle, a wonderful hunter. . . . He cut hardwood, and he and his wife made strips for baskets. They made their own dyes and dyed some of the wood, using tree roots, onions, juniper bark and so on for their colours, and made baskets. Used an ordinary rowboat, not a canoe, dried moose hide and made "moose shanks" moccasins. . . . [They] had a garden. They caught meat and fish and smoked it in their smokehouse. . . . Mrs. Lonecloud was also a nice person.

Katie Mailman Rumley, another neighbour of the Lonecloud family, mentioned to Legge that she used to pick flowers with their daughter Libby. "Lonecloud's daughter could walk so quietly that one minute she'd be picking flowers way across the field, and next she'd be right beside you and you never heard her coming." [13]

Walter Baker of Little Liscomb recalled that his grandfather had been out hunting one night with Lonecloud and had hurt his foot. Baker said that Lonecloud went nine miles up the river, in the dark, and found the kinds of plants that he needed to make medicine for the wounded foot. As a result, it healed well. [14] In other expeditions, Lonecloud served as a guide for Americans who came to hunt moose and caribou in the area.

Clearly, Lonecloud and his family lived fairly happily at Liscomb. Thus it seemed strange that Lonecloud did not discuss this period of his life with either Clara Dennis or Harry Piers. However, Blake Conrad, a researcher for the Treaty and Aboriginal Rights Centre, Shubenacadie, has shed light on this mystery. Jerry Lonecloud evidently had an affair with a married woman while her husband was away working in the woods, and she too had a son by him. This incident caused stress in his own marriage,

Liscomb Mills in the early twentieth century. The Lonecloud family had a frame house near here, but its remains are buried under Liscomb Lodge.
(NSM, N-15,632)

and Lonecloud separated from Elizabeth, at least for a while, leaving Liscomb about 1909 or 1910. They seem to have reunited at some point, but Jerry kept in touch with his other son and often returned to take him hunting. This boy's grandchildren, named Langille, still live in the area.[15]

From 1910 until his death in 1930, Lonecloud moved among various locations in Halifax County. Piers lists him as living in Enfield in 1910, at Tufts Cove near Dartmouth from 1914 to 1918, at Truro and Elmsdale in 1919, at Armdale in 1922, at Old Chapel, Mumford Road, Halifax, in 1923, and at Miller's Lake in 1926. He was back in Halifax by February 1927. During this time, he served both as a respected leader of his own people and as a valuable source of information about native culture.

Harry Piers frequently alluded to Lonecloud's intelligence. He said that Lonecloud was "possessed of a fund of information on matters dealing with his race. . . . I always found him frank, loyal, and he had a razor-keen sense of humour. He was familiar with every brook, river and lake from Windsor to Canso. He could outline the course of a river from memory, tracing its turns without fail." Fifteen years after Lonecloud's death, Haligonian William C. Borrett recorded vivid memories of the man: "With his greying hair, tied in neat little pigtails, and with gay ribbons woven into the end of the braids, he was generally to be seen for a few days of each week wandering about the streets of the city." He added that he was "quite a power in the tribe."[16]

Lonecloud sought justice for the Mi'kmaw people by petitioning the local Indian agent, Angus Boyd, and officials in the Department of Indian Affairs, Ottawa; Piers drafted letters for him, and these drafts remain in the Nova Scotia Museum. A number of these letters were appeals for assistance in securing native property rights. For example, a Jacob Gilby claimed ownership of a piece of land on a Mi'kmaw reserve on the Shubenacadie River, close to Elmsdale, and refused to allow the people to plant crops there. In his third letter to the Department regarding this issue, dated July 17, 1916, Lonecloud argued against the Department's support for Gilby's claims and provided specific evidence to back up his position. The final portion of the letter is compelling:

> Now surely this very long possession by these Indians of these lands must at least give them a title to the ground as "squatters," as in the case with white men, although we Indians distinctly do not like the term "squatters" applied to us, when we consider that the whole lands of the Province once were our own. However, failing other recognized rights, we feel that we can at least clearly claim this particular property by what you term squatters rights, and we urge and expect you to see that our rights, of whatever kind, are duly respected. A meeting of this tribe will take place at the Shubenacadie Reservation on 26th July, when this matter will be brought up, and the Indians are very much dissatisfied with the condition of affairs. We hope that you will see that justice is due us. Members of our tribe are serving at this point in the Empire's cause [World War I], and we desire that all due consideration be shown us. Your obedient servant, Jerry Lone Cloud.[17]

In three letters, written in March, April, and November, 1917, Lonecloud asked repeatedly for help in moving Mi'kmaw families in the Tufts Cove settlement to the Spring Brook reserve near Shubenacadie.[18] He pointed out to the Department that funds actually owed to these Mi'kmaw families from the sale of timber on their lands could be applied towards this assistance. In other words, they were not simply asking for a handout.

> *Tufts Cove, Dartmouth, N.S.*
> *20th March, 1917*

To the Secretary, Department of Indian Affairs, Ottawa.
The petition of the undersigned Micmac Indians of Halifax County, Nova Scotia, at present located at Tufts Cove, Elmsdale and Enfield, humbly sheweth: That we intend to move with our families during the coming spring of 1917 to the Indian Reservation at Spring Brook near Shubenacadie, Nova Scotia, and we request that such monies coming to us from the sale of the timber on the Indian lands at Ship Harbour, Halifax Co., be applied by your department to the erection of suitable dwelling-houses for us and our families at the said Spring Brook Reservation near Shubenacadie.

> *Tufts Cove, Dartmouth N.S.*
> *9 April 1917*

To the Secretary, Department of Indian Affairs, Ottawa.
Sir, By petition to you dated 20th March of this year, certain Indians of Tufts Cove, Elmsdale & Enfield, N.S., requested that moneys coming to them for sale of timber on Indian lands at Ship Harbour, Halifax County, be applied to the erection of dwelling-houses for them at the Indian Reservation at Spring Brook near Shubenacadie, N.S., to which place they wish to move this spring in order to begin to cultivate the soil there. No reply has been received to that petition and meantime the season is rapidly passing, and the cost of provisions being much higher, which will bring distress to many of the Indian families, particularly those at Tufts Cove. Four families at Tufts Cove, namely the families of Frank Brooks, Joe Brooks, Jim Brooks & Jerry Lone Cloud, desire to locate at Shubenacadie as soon as possible, or else the season will be too late to plant. . . . We also beg that speedy consideration be given to our petition of

the 20th March, and that it is not allowed to lie undealt with until it is too late to be of material assistance. I have the honour to be, Sir, Your obedient servant, Jerry Lone Cloud.

Lonecloud apparently received no reply to either of these letters. Seven months later, the situation became even more urgent, as the native people at Tufts Cove were threatened with another crisis over property rights: eviction in two weeks' time. Therefore, he wrote again:

> *Tufts Cove, Dartmouth, N.S.*
> *27 November 1917*
>
> Secretary, Department of Indian Affairs, Ottawa.
> Sir, since time out of mind, members of the Micmac Tribe have camped on ground near Tufts Cove, a little north of the Brewery, on the east side of Halifax Harbour, where there is also situated an Indian school house. This camping ground is claimed by Mr. Farrell of Halifax, and notice has been given the Indians to remove within two weeks. The Indians claim that although this land is not a reservation, yet they have surely rights there by long occupation, even if it be regarded only in the light of what is termed squatter's rights. We claim that we should not therefore be pressed to leave; and that if we do leave, it should be by mutual arrangement between the Indians and Mr. Farrell, and by the payment of money in order that we relinquish our rights. Some of the Indians are willing to remove, while others of the older families hold to what they consider to be their rights, and desire compensation if they leave the place. We desire that your Department will promptly render us assistance and protection in this matter, as we are unable to do much by ourselves without due backing from the Department. I have the honour to be, Sir, Your obedient servant, Jerry Lone Cloud. Tufts Cove, Dartmouth.

Lonecloud's petitions again fell on deaf ears; his requests were never acted upon, his letters were apparently never acknowledged, and the Mi'kmaw people were not assisted in their efforts to move from Tufts Cove. On

The Trade and Labour Council Bazaar at the Armouries, Halifax, 13 October 1924. Jerry Lonecloud is at the left, the child is Nancy Paul, and the basketmaker is Mrs. Joe Brooks of Truro. (NSM, N-6104)

December 6, 1917, ten days after the last petition was sent off, the ships *Imo* and *Mont Blanc* collided in Halifax Harbour in the Narrows opposite Tufts Cove. The *Mont Blanc* was loaded with ammunition, and the resulting explosion completely destroyed the little Mi'kmaw settlement, along with much of northern Halifax and Dartmouth. On December 31, Lonecloud told Piers the poignant details of this tragedy, which had struck him personally: his daughters Rosie and Hannah were both killed.

> Many of the Indians had gone down near the shore to see the steamer on fire and were there when the explosion took place. Pieces of iron were hurled about them. The settlement consisted of seven shanties in the spruce woods there. These shanties were destroyed. There were 21 Indians in the settlement, of whom 9

were killed instantly or afterwards died from injuries received and 12 escaped but were mostly badly injured. . . . Rosie, daughter of Jerry Lone Cloud, had been pinned beneath timbers, but not instantly killed. She asked that she might see a priest. She died later. The Relief Committee is building houses for the surviving Indians near the school-house adjoining the late settlement. They have received food, clothing and shelter from the Dartmouth Committee. Jerry Lone Cloud was at Kentville, N.S., at time of the explosion, but he immediately returned on a relief train, and reached Dartmouth that evening by walking all the way from Windsor Junction. His wife was also absent, in south-eastern New Brunswick. Lone Cloud himself is at present quartered at 145 Upper Water Street, Halifax.[19]

Rosie, Hannah and four others were buried in a common grave in the Dartmouth Roman Catholic cemetery on December 20, with Father Underwood officiating. Jerry and Elizabeth's third daughter, Mary Anne, had died earlier in the war, as Elizabeth set down in a sad little note written to her nephew Abram Paul, who lay convalescing in an English hospital after being gassed in the trenches.[20] Of her eight children, only Libby, Jerry, and Louis remained.

Jerry Lonecloud refused to be defeated by the tragic loss of his children. He continued to serve as a leader for the Mi'kmaq; for example, he advocated for changes in game laws in order to allow Indians to hunt for their own sustenance in closed season. He served as Captain and then as Sub-Chief before becoming Chief of the Mi'kmaq of Halifax County. He also received a unique title: Chief Medicine Man for Halifax County, a title that was later extended to include all of Nova Scotia as well as Prince Edward Island.[21] It is not quite clear by whom this title was conferred.

At the same time that he was advocating for his people, Jerry Lonecloud was interpreting Mi'kmaw culture, language, and legends to non-natives. On August 25, 1910, he had made his first recorded visit to the Provincial Museum of Nova Scotia, bringing to Harry Piers, the renowned curator of the museum, a stone adze. On September 27, he returned with another stone adze, and from then on, Piers and Lonecloud became friends and colleagues.

Mi'kmaw woman's suspender tabs, made in 1860 by Marie Louise Paul Cope, Ship Harbour, and collected in 1913 by Jerry Lonecloud. (NSM)

Over the next twenty years, he brought Piers close to two hundred Mi'kmaw artifacts and items of natural history. His finds for Piers included historic photographs of Mi'kmaw people, strips of dried moose-meat, sweetgrass baskets, quill-work boxes, and *waltes* games, as well as a magnificent beadwork and ribbon-appliqué suspender tab, the best one of its kind in any collection. Lonecloud provided the museum with specimens of a variety of birds, beasts and fish, edible plants, natural dyes, and native tobaccos. Most of these are still valued museum holdings, although some items, such as samples of food, no longer survive. Whenever he brought his finds in to the museum, he told Piers stories about his life and his heritage, which Piers carefully recorded.

Among Lonecloud's most important contributions to the museum were the oral histories he gave Piers about the Mi'kmaq. Very few pre-twentieth-century accounts or documents survive which mention individual Mi'kmaw people by name, and even fewer tell anything personal about an individual. Thus every time Piers recorded one of Lonecloud's oral histories, a few more people and their lives were rescued from oblivion. For example, he told Piers about an incident related to him in 1874 by a woman whom he thought was a hundred years old. Piers wrote:

A Micmac Indian, known as Dr. Lone Cloud or Jerry Bartlett, informs me that about 1874, a very old Indian woman, Magdalene Pennall of Sissiboo, Weymouth, Digby County, informed him that there had then been long known to her people certain very large rib-bones which they supposed to be "whale ribs," on the barrens about two or three miles south-eastward of Blue Mountain Lake, about twenty-five miles from the sea, in the northeastern part of Yarmouth county, N.S. The place is a very short distance east of Bloody Creek or brook (a tributary of the Clyde River) and on a trail from that creek via Long Lake, to the headwaters of the Shelburne or Roseway river to the eastward. On one occasion, Mrs. Pennall and her husband Joe Kophang, just after having left their canoe on Bloody Creek, killed a moose at the spot where the bones were, and as a thundershower came on, they stood three of the large ribs against a rock, covered them with the moosehide, and so formed a shelter. Some of the ribs which were on the ground were covered with a thick mantle of moss. Lone Cloud thinks there may have been some vertebrae there also, but knew of no other kinds of bones. Once some Indian carried away one of these big ribs, but as it was very heavy, it was at last dropped, and the Indians affirmed that it was afterwards found once more in its original place, which caused the remains to be regarded with veneration by numbers of the tribe.[22]

This account is rich with information. Two people previously lost in time have been recovered: Madeleine Bernard (pronounced Penal in Mi'kmaq), probably born in the eighteenth century, and her husband, Joe Kophang, whose last name may either be a Mi'kmaw word or the French name Copain. Their home territory and land-use patterns, their portage routes, are given. The suggestion that the bone-place became a power site because the bones "walked" sheds light on customs and world view. The discovery of what Piers felt was a fossilized mastodon, not a whale, is naturally of great interest. But what is more important, because of its rarity, is the glimpse we have of an event in Mi'kmaw lives two centuries past: Madeleine and Joe sitting under a mastodon-and-moosehide tent, perhaps roasting meat and licking the fat off their fingers, while a thunderstorm roars overhead, on a day when the hunting had been good. This is priceless knowledge, data that could have been obtained in no other way. It is a lost past, flashing for a moment into vivid life.

From 1923 through 1929, Jerry Lonecloud did more to preserve such memories. He dictated a lengthy and much more detailed memoir to Clara Dennis, the Nova Scotia journalist and writer. In hours of interviews

Jerry Lonecloud selling baskets in Halifax, drawn in pastels by D.C. MacKay, November 1928. (NSM, N-10,680)

with her, he described portions of his own life, including his time as a showman and his role as a "medicine man." He also provided descriptions of Mi'kmaw culture as he had lived it and related Mi'kmaw legends as he had heard them. This material, in his own words, is presented in succeeding chapters.

By 1929, when he gave his last interviews, Lonecloud was about seventy-five years old. Blind in one eye, his sight in the other eye failing, he still went about the city, a familiar figure to all, leaning on his cane. Harry Piers had his portrait made one last time that year, on February 2. On April 15, 1930, Jerry Lonecloud was suddenly taken sick. It was a short but severe illness. He was admitted to the Victoria General Hospital in Halifax, and on the following day, Harry Piers recorded Lonecloud's death in his journal:

> Wednesday, April 16. Cold. My old Micmac Indian friend, "Dr." Jeremiah Lone-cloud, died this morning, after about 24 hours illness, aged about 78 or 79 years. He had been in to see me about Saturday of last week. I have known him well for about 20 years. I really felt quite badly at his passing.[23]

Two days later, at 2:30 p.m. on April 18, Lonecloud was buried in St. Peter's Roman Catholic cemetery, Dartmouth, near where his daughters Rosie and Hannah were interred.

And what of Jerry and Elizabeth Lonecloud's surviving children? Harald Prins, professor at Kansas State University, has discovered a 1936 newspaper photograph of Libby Lonecloud and Henry Perley, a Maliseet.[24] The caption says that both of them were then living at Moose Head Lake, New York; Henry is identified as "Red Eagle" and Libby as "Princess Lone Cloud." Evidently Libby was carrying on the family tradition of appearing in medicine shows. According to people in the Liscomb area, she had long black hair that fell to her ankles and was very beautiful. Libby's brother Louis died in 1931, at the age of twenty-two, and was buried in the Sacred Heart Cemetery at Millbrook. Elizabeth herself was buried next to Louis thirty years later, in 1961. Young Jerry is reported to have descendants still living in Nova Scotia, as does Lonecloud's son by the Liscomb woman.

Lonecloud's great-grandson, Harvey Boutilier, has lately added to our

Jerry Lonecloud and Elizabeth Paul's oldest daughter, Rosie Bartlett MacDonald, with one of her three children. Rosie was married to "Indian Jim" MacDonald of Sherbrooke Village. (NSM, Sherbrooke Village, N-7608)

knowledge of his family.[25] Harvey's grandmother was Rosie Macdonald, Lonecloud's oldest child, who was killed in the Halifax Explosion of 1917. Rosie and her husband, Jim MacDonald, of Sherbrooke, had three children: Harvey, Murray, and Mary Elizabeth (named for her maternal grandmother). Mary Elizabeth, who was three years old at the time, was badly burned in the explosion, and so was her brother Murray.

According to Boutilier, the Halifax YMCA was turned into a burn unit, and a Dr. Codmen came from Massachusetts with ten other doctors, nine nurses, and four "civilians," to help out. He treated Mary Elizabeth. When she was considered well enough to discharge, after many months of pain, arrangements were made to put her in St. Joseph's orphanage. Her brothers, aged fourteen and twelve, came with her to place her there. She never again saw them or any other members of her family. She lived at the orphanage until she was old enough to go out to work. She married her first employer, Myles Burton Boutilier, a widower from Tantallon, Nova Scotia. Their son Harvey was named after Mary Elizabeth's brother.

During his visit to the Nova Scotia Museum, Harvey Boutilier was shown a photograph of Rosie, his grandmother, the first he had ever seen, and of other members of the family. When photos of Lonecloud were brought out, the physical resemblance between Harvey and his great-grandfather was striking. Clearly, Harvey Boutilier is a living memorial to his ancestor.

Thus, Jerry Lonecloud lives on through his descendants. He also survives in the memories of those whose lives he touched. Ruth Legge of Liscomb puts it this way: "Lonecloud walks the place, they say. Lonecloud walks the place." Perhaps, however, the most important way that Lonecloud lives on is through his own words, spoken to Clara Dennis and to Harry Piers. These are his legacy to future generations of natives and non-natives alike.

Clara Dennis took this photograph of Jerry Lonecloud in her garden at 45 Coburg Road, Halifax, between 1923 and 1929. The house is no longer standing. (NSM, N-14,803)

TWO
Here's What I Remember:
The Memoir of Jerry Lonecloud

THE MI'KMAQ HAVE *two forms of stories: the* aknutmaqn, *literally meaning "he tells news"; and the* a'tukwaqn, *a more mythic style of story that is passed on from one generation to the next and often told for entertainment. Here are the aknutmaqn tales, Jerry Lonecloud telling news, telling what he remembered.*

First, he tells of his life and something of his father's experiences in the American Civil War. These stories allow insight into what the world was like for a Mi'kmaw man born into the nineteenth century and living into the twentieth. They show how much of his Mi'kmaw heritage he retained and the extent of his adaptation to the dominant culture. They also shed a revealing light on older Mi'kmaw customs: courting and marriage, the duties of hus- band and wife, proper behaviour for children, the role of a medicine man.

Much of the information Lonecloud passed on to Clara Dennis is not documented anywhere else. As an example, he preserved such customs as "wish-bone" (shoulder-blade) divination. This practice was part of the lives of other Algonquian-speakers, such as the Cree, but until Dennis wrote down Lonecloud's words, there was no documented evidence that the Mi'kmaq, too, used this method of foretelling the future. Lonecloud talks of tracking and hunting and the treatment of bones after the kill. The place names he mentions, and the names of stars, of healing medicines, of birds and beasts, all greatly enrich modern knowledge of traditional Mi'kmaw culture.

Lonecloud saved much that was thought to be lost forever, from the most profound beliefs to the simple things of everyday life: birth, sickness, old age, and death; women washing clothes and bringing in fresh water every morn- ing, just as the sun rises. He left a picture of life going on, his aknutmaqn passing cultural memories into the future.

Through Jerry Lonecloud, the Mi'kmaw people speak: "We have lived here since the world began. They say we came from places like China or the Bering Strait. But we know where we come from — we come from this very place. . . . And this is who we are."   *R.H.W.*

I Was Brought Up Among Medicine People

I was born in Belfast, Maine, on the mouth of the Penobscot River. My father and mother, they were Mi'kmaq from Nova Scotia, and they was medicine people. My mother and father were both medicine people and doctored among the white people. They made the medicine.

Each tribe has one medicine man. His wife would be the medicine woman. With their families, they travelled and treated people of different villages. I was brought up among them. All of them wintered together up some rivers of the Great Lakes. In those days, people believed in the Indian medicine. And doctors were pretty scarce, not so plentiful as now.

My father and my uncle took me to the woods, showed me how to gather plants and taught me to distinguish plants. Mussikonn, the first archbishop of French town in Digby County, twenty miles the other side of Weymouth, taught Latin to my father and my uncle. My father and my uncle sang in church at Eel Brook chapel, near Tusket.

My father and grandfather were both medicine men. When we were in Boston, Father was a herb doctor for Morse's pills. Father was in with Morse. Morse got rich on it, and he called it Morse's Indian Root Pills. Father was the Indian. He gave the fellow the secret. That fellow got rich, but they fell out. Father left and branched off by himself.

In those times we didn't care about earning a living because we could get our living in the streams.

Six of these medicine people went up the Great Lakes and in the rivers, in Lake Superior. Always camped in the woods when we was travelling, and lived on wild animals while we were getting herbs. We had good chances to get our game. There were four or five big canoes, and we travelled the waters of the Great Lakes and wintered up in the rivers, hunting. In summer, we'd go in little towns and villages, treating people

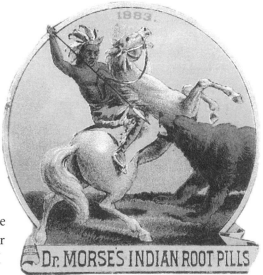

Chromolithographed medicine-bottle label. "Dr. Morse's Indian Root Pills" were prepared and sold by Lonecloud's father, in partnership with Dr. Morse. (Collection of Joe Nickell. Photo: Tom Flynn.)

Dr. MORSE'S INDIAN ROOT PILLS

with medicine. We stayed at the French settlement eighteen or twenty miles behind Quebec. I grew up this way.

At Traverse Bay, Lake Superior, I was not two years old when I had a convulsion. They took me in a canoe and went along down the St. Lawrence River to St. Anne. I was taken to St. Anne and cured. I was also baptized. Baptized Haselma. Haselilia, that's my sister.

Those medicine people travelled together for four or five years, travelled the lakes and came down to Kahnawake, about thirteen miles above Montreal. Kahnawake Mohawk don't speak like us. All Algonquian languages like Mi'kmaq are similar to each other, but the Iroquois language is different. We can't swear in Mi'kmaq in any form or another. In our language, there is not one cuss word. All we know about swearing is what we get from the French and English.

We were in Kahnawake with those medicine people for a number of years and then parted. We separated, and my family — we was Laksis — went up Lake Champlain to Grand Isle. This was about sixty years ago. Sixty years ago. Two groups of us was on Lake Champlain. One family took one side, and the other, another. We treated the villages and met at Grand Isle during the winter. Yep. We went in a few years to Lake Champlain.

From here I remember — my next memory is these songs. We had a song:

Get out the way, Alan Tucker,
You're too late for your supper.
This week for the waggon,
We'll all take a ride.

One time we went by way of the Erie Canal four hundred miles to New York. People used to go on boats with cattle. We covered the distance and camped in Brooklyn, where the Brooklyn Bridge is now, in an alder swamp. Every time I smell the smoke of the alder, it reminds me of that time. I was then six or seven. I am seventy-two now.

Then we went up the river and back again, and then to Lake Champlain. We stayed on Grand Isle. It's twelve miles long, in Lake Champlain. We stayed there for eight years. Done basket work and made herb medicine. There were just two canoes there, two families. This was about sixty years ago. They doctored there until my father went to the American Civil War in 1860 or '61.

Father Went to the American Civil War

He enlisted in Plattsburg, New York. Fought with the Americans three years and come through all right. When Father came back after serving three years, people were being drafted. And Father took another man's place. Henry Lovell from North Hero, Grand Isle, Vermont, this was. Henry paid Father five hundred dollars to take his place. My mother lived on this war money.

The war ended. Father was one of the eighteen men from a New York regiment who volunteered to capture Booth, who shot Abraham Lincoln. There was a big reward to capture him. It was one hundred thousand dollars, to be divided among the eighteen, but the officers were probably going to get the most.

Father was one of the eighteen men who captured Booth. Shot him in the leg. Then they took him off on a gunboat way off to sea, tied a grindstone to his neck, and threw him overboard. So my father, Abram Laksi, told me. My father and a white man approached the barn where Booth was hiding in a hay mow. Orders were given to give himself up. They knew he was in the barn, for he had eaten his supper at the house. Booth refused to give himself up. My father and the other man both fired into the hay mow, and one of their bullets struck Booth in the thigh. Booth said, "Don't fire any more. I give myself up." He was then captured and taken back.

My father told me they took Booth in one of them old fashioned man-of-war boats. Took him off out to sea alive, tied a grindstone to his neck, and put him overboard, way off the coast of Virginia. Killing any other way was too good. "They wouldn't give him the honour to hang him," said Father. They wouldn't give him an inch of land. Put a grindstone around his neck while there was life in him. They did it at night. Wouldn't give him the honour of publishing it, having it known.

After the Booth affair, Father came back home. While he was gone, my mother had moved to Waterbury, Vermont, and Father came there. He and I went out in the woods with bows and arrows. He shot a deer. Then he told me all about the war and that he was going to New York to draw his share of the hundred thousand dollar reward money. He went a few days later, as he was anxious to get the money. We were to return to our home in Nova Scotia. Father drew his money, and we never saw or heard of him again. Blacklegs got him, we think, and killed him and robbed him. None of his people ever knew. Mother wrote on to the authorities, but they replied he had drawn his money and that was all they knew.

My mother died that spring, the same year the war ended. Same spring as Father died, Mother died in Waterbury, Vermont. We were in Water-bury, Vermont, on the Onion River, and were waiting for Father to bring the money. Here Mother died. She died in April. The war had ended in the first part of the winter. She left four children. There were four of us then. Two died later. My sister, Sarah Michael, is still alive. She married an Indian and is living in Bear River. I was oldest, twelve or thirteen years old.

My mother was Mary Ann Tomah from Windsor, Nova Scotia. Mother told us about her home in Nova Scotia. She told us about her place at St. Margaret's Bay — where the hydro-electric land is now, where the mill is and the electric plant. Mother's father had bought it, and Mother was his only heir.

William and Madeleine Prosper, about 1909, at Tufts Cove, Dartmouth. William, a cooper, died in 1923, at the age of 101. He knew Jerry Lonecloud's maternal grandfather and mother well. (NSM, N-5572)

Mother's father was a trapper. Beaver skins were balanced against silver — beaver skin on the one side and silver on the other. Before silk was thought of and before silk worm had took possession, hats were made of beaver. William Prosper, ninety-seven years old, from Truro, remembers my mother and grandfather. He lived with them all one winter.

We Then Started for St. Margaret's Bay

We took the Vermont Central Railway to Boston, and then we got on a paddle boat, the *City of Richmond*, for Saint John, New Brunswick. The young ones got too seasick, and we got off at Portland, Maine, and stayed at Cape Elizabeth.

There was a camping ground of Maliseet Indians at Cape Elizabeth, and here we stayed two months. We stayed until Portland was burnt up, July 4, 1866 or 1867. All that was left was the post office, and many lost their lives. While we were there, I used to go to Castine, Maine, and see the kerosene and glass lamps being made. It was wonderful when they blowed the glass to make lamps and lampshades. I used to go to see the kerosene made. It was the greatest thing. About four miles from there were the great paper mills, and I used to go to see them, too.

In Maine, we met Mother's relations from Nova Scotia. One Mi'kmaw woman from Nova Scotia came while we were living at Cape Elizabeth. She advised us to live with her because they were going back home next summer. We went with them. The whole four of us took the boat when it came around again and went to Belfast, Maine. We camped out at Bucksport, Maine.

Next summer, they bought a little sailboat to go along the shore with, and the old Indians built two canoes. I and one of the old Indians occupied one canoe, and the family, the big boat and the other canoe. Me and the old Indian went ahead and selected camping grounds along the coast. We finally reached Grand Manan. Here we remained two or three weeks, then went to Brier Island in the canoe.

We landed at Brier Island, Digby County, in a canoe. We canoed from Grand Manan to Brier Island, forty miles. We could not see across. Me and the old man in the canoe, we got to Brier Island, but the others — in the boat — stopped at Yarmouth. We went in the woods hunting and built another canoe. I went on to Yarmouth in that canoe in the fall of the year. The others were cooking dinner at a brook and getting some trout. I went out to look around, and I saw some withrod berries.

From the time we first left home, it took me nearly two years to reach Nova Scotia.

Musmaya'l — Monsieur Maillard

For a long time, I lived up in the woods with an old man, Saln. That's Charles in Indian. Saln. Peter Charles. Up Carleton Lake. Old Peter Charles lived there. Up this lake is Kluskap's weir. No trout, no gaspereaux or salmon, no kind of fish would ever be here unless we honoured Kluskap. Kluskap's dogs are here at Forest Glen, *L'mu'juiktuk,* but can't be seen. *L'mu'juiktuk* means "at the dogs." Kluskap's dogs are called *mootcoolay-senmuek,*[*1] Mi'kmaw dogs. It means "the dog will lay down and cross his paws one over another." Old Peter Charles. I cared for him until he died. Then I buried him at Eel Brook. He taught me lots of things.

Peter Charles told me the story of Musmaya'l, a French priest. Musmaya'l — Monsieur Maillard — first taught the Indians at *Pankwenopskuk,* meaning lice-picking falls. Now they call it Gabriel's Falls.

Three miles from Tusket Village, at the foot of Gabriel's Falls, there is a big rock. There is a story about a mermaid coming and taking away some young girls who were playing on this rock. They were hunting one another's heads for lice, and they were told they mustn't go there any more. But they went anyway, and a mermaid took them away. They have never been seen since. This happened many hundreds of years ago. Indians have camped there since. It is a great camping ground because it is a good fishing ground. Monsieur Maillard made his first chapel there, at Pankwenop-skuk, "where they hunt one another's head."

Monsieur Maillard came from France before the Revolutionary War, when the French were on the good side of the Indians. He brought beads to wear and also prayer beads. All the Indians from the Carleton River around Tusket and Tusket Forks, from Little Bad Falls where there was a great encampment, and from Mispaw, about three miles from Little Bad Falls, would come for the services. Some came as far as forty miles. At Pankwenopskuk, he erected a bark *pqa'wi'kan,* meaning "a camp made of spruce rinds." The bark is outside, rinds is next. Rinds is next to the bark, the thick part on the inside. He made a chapel out of spruce bark. Peter Charles told me this.

When the first English people came up to Gabriel's Falls, they fired at the Indians, and the Indians took to their canoes and went away elsewhere.

Next the Indians took the French priest in canoes to *Penatkuk*, "bird-nesting place," an island in the Shelburne River. Here they made another bark pqa'wi'kan, a wigwam chapel or rind camp to hold services. It was called the St. Anne's Mission. Indians would come here from Indian Gardens, Kejimkujik. They would come through the woods and by canoe. They could come from the Clyde River and the Barrington River a good ways, forty or fifty miles.

Musmaya'l,
"Monsieur Maillard."
Abbé Pierre Antoine Simon Maillard ministered in Nova Scotia from 1734 to 1761.

The St. Anne's Mission was later rebuilt of wood and has since rotted down. A cross made of oak is still on an island where they used to bury their dead. It is a little island off Penatkuk, the island with the Shelburne River on both sides. This island is near Lower Ohio. You can get a boat or snowshoes and go over to the island and find that cross.

Next the Indians went with the priest up Roseway Lake by the way of Tobeatic, to Indian Gardens. Monsieur Maillard stayed there and converted the Indians. He found many Indians there. There is no cross there, only a cross carved on a rock near the Club House on Fairy Lake. There's a graveyard in the dead of the woods, among great trees — hemlock, grey birch, white birch, pines, spruce — and there are a number of headstones with no mark. Only one headstone has a cross cut in it. Mi'kmaq here always sewed their dead in birchbark — to keep them together, I guess. Birchbark would last for hundreds of years. It does not rot like wood.

You want to go and see our old dead peoples? John Canon, a guide, had a little bungalow on the left side of the road what goes out to Minard's. Well, go between John Canon's and Minard's on the left hand side of the road going in. The Indian graveyard is off the main road.

The priest stayed a long while at Indian Gardens. Then he was taken by the Indians to Halifax at the Narrows. Old John Morris said that at the narrowest part of the Narrows there was a huge pine tree. When the Indians heard the priest was coming, they climbed the tree and hoisted a skin on a pole for a signal. It was a great time. The missionary was there for a couple of years, but he did not build a chapel. He said another priest was to come. Which of course was true.

Jerry Lonecloud in 1920, with a birchbark cross made as a memorial to Major-General Campbell Hardy, who died in 1919. Campbell Hardy had hunted with Lonecloud's grandfather, Tom Phillips.
(NSM, N-5492)

He done great work there, got 'em all christened, changed their names. . . . They all got christened but one Indian. This fellow's name was Peter Saln, Peter Charles. He said he did not want his name changed, but so many got at him that he finally agreed. The priest wouldn't go until he had every one christened.

The priest would come around the camps to see they denied themselves on Friday — no meat. He would look in camps very early Friday mornings to see if they were cooking meat. One day he came to the last man he had christened and found him cooking meat. Priest said, "I told you to deny yourself and not eat meat Fridays. You're cooking meat here. Didn't I tell you not to cook nor eat meat on Friday? And you've just been christened."

"Huh," says the old man. "This ain't meat. It's fish. I done this like you done me. I put salt on it and water on it and named it Halibut." Indians would spear halibut.

The priest said, "That's all very well now, but don't you christen your meat any more."

After this, Monsieur Maillard went to Ship Harbour, to *Wayelgwask*,* "head of the lake." Built another pqa'wi'kan at Indian Point. Here he converted more of the Indians from Jeddore, Musquodoboit, Tangier. They all flocked in as from other places. Here he christened the Indians. Word had gone ahead, and the Indians, they all believed in the priest.

Next he went to St. Mary's. He went to the Forks at Melrose, nine miles from Sherbrooke. There's an island in the East River not a mile from St. Mary's Forks, and he established another St. Anne's or pqa'wi'kan there. The name of the island on which that chapel was built was *Nimnoqinuk*, which means "big grey birch." That birch was eight foot through, twenty-four foot around. It has been there many hundreds of years and is still standing about two miles above the Forks. You can drive up to it. Go by way of Glenelg. Anyone in St. Mary's will tell you where it is. There is also a cross of oak that has fallen down but still exists. The old Indians camped near it. Monsieur Maillard was at St. Mary's for quite a length of time. He was well liked.

The next place he went was *Poqmkek*. Means "at the straight river." At Heatherton, twenty miles from Antigonish, between it and Port Hawksbury. Here he established his last St. Anne. Then he visited some of the old

Abbé Maillard was buried in old St. Paul's cemetery, Spring Garden Road, Halifax. Mi'kmaq, Acadian, and English all attended his funeral. His grave is not marked, and its whereabouts within the cemetery is unknown.

places he had performed services. He ended his days among the Indians in Halifax, but Indians don't know where he was buried.

I Lived Around Yarmouth

Took in hunting, and I was a game guide for sportsmen from the U.S. and also Yarmouth people. I have a little island at English Mill Lake. They still call it Jerry's Island. I used to camp there when I was hunting, for years and years. Hunting for beavers, bears, wildcats, otters. Went to it first when I was living with old Peter Charles. The French people named it Jerry's Island. There's a good landing place, much hardwood, and a hill on the island. A nice round hill and a large wigwam. Very pretty island.

In Yarmouth, Mrs. Jacob Bingay asked me to work for her. She gave me $1.25 for my day's work. This was the first money I had ever had. Mrs. Joseph Bond, the doctor's wife, gave me another day's work. People used to be paid in food, clothing, dishes, and presents. They were just as well satisfied then.

For a while, I was boss for the ton timber for shipbuilding in Tusket. Timber for ships went by the ton. At Bad Falls, I ran two rafts abreast through the Bad Falls at the Gulch at Carleton or about a mile above Carleton. This was the first time that had been done. No one ever dared to do it, it was so narrow. Very dangerous. I was the first man to run through Smith's Pitch at the head of Bad Falls on a single log. Pitch is about eight feet. I never got washed off. They thought it couldn't be done. I showed them, and it's been done ever since. Quite daring awful. Some folks may see this up there, and they'll remember. The old folks will tell the young ones.

I lived around Yarmouth for twenty years. Then I returned to the U.S. My sister stayed in Nova Scotia.

Mi'kmaw moose call, made of birchbark by Jerry Lonecloud, 12 October 1915, while living at Elmsdale, Nova Scotia. He sold it to the Provincial Museum for twenty-five cents. (NSM)

I Was a Showman

There was a man around named John E. Healey, from the States. Hiring Indians for the Kickapoo Medicine Company. He was to hire all the Indians he could. He come to Bear River, but he got only three of us. I made an appointment to go with him a certain day. He wanted to hire Indians for the Kickapoo Indian Medicine Company that was getting up in Park Square, Boston. He offered us seven dollars a week and clothes. We had to dress up in Indian clothes, buckskin and feathers. And board and expenses paid back and forth guaranteed. He left money in John Dohey's in Digby for our passage if we went on board.

At this time I was still living with Governor-Chief Jim Meuse at Bear River. He was called Governor-Chief because his father, André Meuse, was the first Mi'kmaw Indian who went to see Queen Victoria just after she was crowned. The Queen called him Governor-Chief and addressed him so, and he was always so-called. Jim was likewise so-called when he became chief. He called himself Governor-Chief also.

Before I left for Boston, I thought I'd get a bunch of trout to take with me. So I went in the woods to a lake called *Ani-matle'nek*, meaning Annie Madeleine's, named after a woman. A companion and I were going. I went to the above lake, and he went to some stream running into the lake. I

Jim Meuse's grandfather was the first to be called the Governor-Chief, after he went to England to see King William and Queen Adelaide. His son André went with him. André returned to England in 1825.

caught quite a bunch of trout, but I wasn't satisfied. I wanted to go to another place to fish. I got onto an Indian path and noticed tracks. Saw it was a bear's track. Bears were cross then in June.

When I saw the fresh tracks, I turned off and ran right into those bears. There were three of them. They made a great noise when they saw me, and I was obliged to go up a spruce tree. Bears are great climbers and could climb better than I, but I planned to go out on a limb.

I looked down. One bear had begun to climb the tree. I swung out onto a limb and across to another tree. As I went from one tree to another, my hat fell off alongside what I shall name the third bear. He immediately tore the hat up and made a noise as if to signal all to depart. As soon as he made the noise, all of them bears ran down towards the river. I did not feel like leaving the tree until I was sure the bears had left the vicinity, even though the blackflies were biting terribly. My trout was left intact by the bears.

My chum had a visit from the bears, too. He ran right into the river. He had his trout in a basket on his back, and he lost them all. He got to the other side of the river eventually.

I said to myself, "It's a good thing I'm going away. There'll be no bears in Boston."

I sold my trout at Boston and got one dollar a pound. I sold them to the Parker House. The manager gave me a dinner on the bargain, also. Then I joined the Kickapoo Medicine Company in Park Square, Boston. I went to work and helped to make the Kickapoo medicine, labeling it and all.

We were sent in the summer through the small towns and in the winter to the halls in big cities. The Kickapoo Company carried big shows free to help sell the medicine. This is the way they advertised it. One or two nights a week they had pay nights. The shows were very good. Some of the show-men were paid as high as forty dollars a week, which was a high salary in those days.

In the show, I lectured, sold medicine, and acted on the stage. All those

Jerry Lonecloud as a young man in Healey and Bigelow's Wild West Show in the 1880s. (NSARM, N-6151)

daring shots. Bursting an apple or a potato by shooting it while it was swinging, cutting a card in two edgeways across the hall. Cutting the card edgeways is a pretty daring shot. You can't see it, but you know where it is. That's a pretty daring shot. I'd shoot and snuff the ashes out of a cigar while it was being smoked. Ain't supposed to use any liquor or tobacco. Keep your nerves steady.

I was a lover of birds, and always in my spare time, I'd be in the woods, shooting.

I separated from the Kickapoo Indian Medicine Show after eight years and formed a company of my own called Kiowa. I trained an Indian girl to do the shooting, and I smoked the cigar. She was very clever. In each town, she won the prize in rifle matches. Snuff the ashes first shot, and her second shot would make the sparks fly out of the same cigar. She would lie down on her back so everything looked upside down. The bullet would come to the block of wood behind me. The audience would be invited to view the block of wood and had the privilege of taking it home, cutting it up, and finding the bullets. The girl would shoot across the hall. It is steadier to shoot that way instead of at arm's length.

Kiowa Indian Company, I called my company. I had eight under me. I had their salaries to pay and halls to rent everywhere. The halls cost all the way from ten dollars to fifty dollars. I paid them all — good as well as bad — fifteen dollars a week. They paid their board, five dollars a week.

I ran the show four years. Then I got in New Hampshire, and business was not so good, so we broke up. My last show was presented at Keene, New Hampshire. The Indian girl White Dove, my crack shot, married Rolling Thunder, and they set up a show of their own. She met him first in my show. He played the violin, and she the piano.

Then I and one of the Pawnee Indians I selected named White Eagle, we joined Buffalo Bill. William F. Cody was Buffalo Bill's name. He was practicing for the Queen's Diamond Jubilee at Madison Square, New York. He carried the Wild West Show, the best show in the world at that time. He was going to play it in the Glass Palace before Queen Victoria. We were at Madison Square four months, all winter, and were to finish off in a month at Coney Island in April.

We had been getting fifteen dollars a week, our board and clothes, tobacco, expenses, everything. We did not have to pay a cent out. After Coney, we were to take the boat for England. Buffalo Bill wanted to cut us down to half-pay while going to England. He told us he was going under a big expense, playing in that Glass Palace.

White Eagle says, "I don't want to go over there." He was hired to go over and couldn't back out very well. "Let's run away," he says to me.

I says, "I don't care about going over there either, since he cut our wages down, and we'll get away." I says, "I think I know a place where we can hide away, and just when they are going down to Coney Island, we'll run away."

We went on the Lehigh Valley railway, and we went into the Catskill Mountains. We camped in the woods, and I used to go out to do the shopping in the county town stores. I used to bring the paper in, so we knew when the show left Coney Island. All this time they were hunting for us. We went back to New York again when it was safe. White Eagle meanwhile was set on marrying a white woman.

I says to White Eagle, "You gonta marry that white squaw?"

"Sure. I won't have to work like I do now." She used to attend the show every night and invite us up to her big house. I stayed awhile with them.

But I got tired of the city. I broke away from them and joined the Kickapoo Company again. I told them I didn't like the city, so they put me with the company out in the towns, like out in Brooklyn. We were performing in Brooklyn near the place where they shut the dead bodies in iron things and roast them until they become ashes and the relatives come and get them. Where they bake them people, you know, iron thing what heats up. Cremates them. This is quite common now.

I don't know how long I was around there, but howsomever, great President Grant died, and there was a funeral, and I went from Buffalo to New York to the funeral. That was greatest sight I ever saw in my life. The train I travelled on from Buffalo was crêped, draped in black crêpe, the cars and the engine, flying white and black. She went out from Buffalo all crêped up. She looked handsome inside and out, all flying in crêpe. We stopped this special express to Pittsburg, Pennsylvania, for twenty minutes for refreshments, and those crêpes were switched off by that time. They put some more on, and this lasted us into Hoboken.

I started to go to the procession on main Broadway, and I couldn't get

Etl-en'tik,
"where it ends."

along with the crowd. Although I was two miles from where he was buried, it was all jammed up, and I never saw the place. All them great buildings, stories high, was crêped around through, and across the streets and everywhere you look. Some million yards of crêpe used that day. The biggest day I ever saw in New York. I couldn't get back nor headways nor sideways and was glad to get into headquarters of Kickapoo after that.

I asked Kickapoo for county towns to go to and was fitted out in county towns in the state of Maine. I stopped there the biggest part of two years. Then I dropped into New York again. They said, "Where'd you like to go now?" I said I'd like to go out to South America and see about that. I stopped there only two months. It was too hot, and I got malaria. Dull country, I found it. I returned to New York, and they sent me out to Brooklyn again. I stayed with that until September first, when I broke away from them and started for New Brunswick.

I got in with an Indian fellow. He told me about hunting at the Richibucto River. I says, "We'll go." And we went and 'twas lovely hunting. Up on Richibucto Stream. Indian name is *Pijipukwaya'si's*. Long narrow straight stream, no crooked in it. The Richibucto River, Indian name *L'sipuktuk*, meaning "dreary river," where it runs into Lonesome Bay.

We stayed all winter, and I caught nineteen beavers on one brook, three otters, one bear, and seven lucifers, which are something like a wildcat. Also martens and caribous. I never counted them because we got them anytime we wanted them. They were in a big bog, lots of them, and we went whenever we wanted one and got them. *Etl-en'tik* is the name of that bog. Means "bog in the fog." You can't see the other end of it; it's like a fog. It is twenty miles long. The head stream goes into the Richibucto River. The stream starts in the bog. There is no lake.

After I left trapping in the spring, I got up a show again. I had medicine and three or four Indians, and we put on a show of old Indian ceremonies like Corn Dance and Medicine Dance. I performed in Chatham, Newcastle, and Fredericton, New Brunswick.

Jerry Lonecloud (right), and Elizabeth Paul, his Maliseet wife, with their travelling medicine show. The canvas tent and stuffed moosehead are props. The other woman and child are unidentified. Sometime after 1890, Lonecloud had this photo printed as a postcard and sent it to his neighbours in Liscomb. (DesBrisay Museum, Bridgewater, Nova Scotia. NSM, N-11,255)

Here I met my wife. I got her for Pocahontas. We showed Pocahontas saving the life of Captain John Smith, and it took well in Saint John, Moncton, Truro, New Glasgow, Pictou, Stellarton, and other different parts of Nova Scotia. I married Pocahontas at Kentville. Elizabeth Paul, only daughter of Louis Paul, the chief at Fredericton. Maliseet tribe. She is a Maliseet. She was seventeen, and I was nearly forty, thirty-seven or more. I liked her ways. There was no more to it. I hired her brother, and she wanted to come. So she did. I stayed at Kentville off and on for two years.

I was a showman.

Some Ways Marriages Are Made

Parents will take one of their oldest boys to a camp where there's girls. Then the old people will be talking about one thing and another like that. The young'uns ain't supposed to talk to one another. The girl would be sitting behind her parents or perhaps lying down. The young man — he'll have a stick perhaps split out or cut with a knife.

This is courtin' now. He would stick the stick in his mouth and bite it to form a dent. So there would be a mark above and below. Then he would throw it so it will hit the girl somewhere. She'll pick that little stick up and give her love marks and throw it back to him. If she doesn't throw it back with a mark on it, there is slender hope for him. If it comes back with another mark of hers on, then it's love. If it comes back with no mark, there's no further conversation, although the old people have a long conversation.

If he receives it with a mark, he bites again. This means a promise and signifies that he'll meet her when she goes after water. Then they can talk the matter over openly between them. He throws it back to her again with this promise. Her answer, when she makes a dent in the stick again, means she will meet him at the point where she gets the water. This settles that. When the time comes for them to meet, then if others see them, they say, "Those two have to get married." And it is already announced when the feast will occur.

After this, they are not supposed to talk to each other until the chief medicine man comes. The parents have already given him notice that the two are going to marry. That night, the young fellow gives his present — whatever he is going to give his sweetheart — to the medicine man, and he gives it to the girl and says where it has come from. It may be fur, shells, or animals' teeth. Beads are made from animals' teeth.

The marriage time is then set — one year or two years, whatever the case may be. Then everyone goes about his business. They meet at the marriage time, and all kinds of food is provided: smoked beaver meat, smoked tongues, smoked eels, salmon, trout. A great feast is held at the wedding.

The chief medicine man marries them. He instructs them, "You have to go away from your parents and leave your parents for yourselves." During this time, the young Indian has selected a certain part of the hunting ground, and he'll bring his wife there. Some part of the lake, some part of the woods, or some part of the river, like that.

Another way marriages are made is with a race. Perhaps one of the oldest chief's daughters, a good many want her. The one that can run the fastest will get her. They start out, quite a few of them, to run for the girl. The fastest runner will get that girl. Perhaps he has not spoken to her before. When he runs the race for her, she says, "I made a wish that you would go the furthest and run the fastest. I saw you before, but never spoke to you, and I've taken a liking to you." This will be the first word between them.

Another way to gain a wife is like this. The old people goes with the boy, and he has got up a great present for the girl, but there's still no talkin' between them. The old people, they bring the present when they meet at night. The old man with the son gives it to the other old man with the daughter, and he gives it to the old lady, who passes it over to the girl. If she keeps it, that means she likes him. If she passes it to her mother again, she means that there is no way she'll accept him.

"What is your fault with the young man?"

She replies, "I've no fault."

The old woman says, "Then you've got to marry him." Then they're forced to marry. Her mother says, "We can't keep you all the time. You've got to go where that present's come from." They are thus forced to be married.

Another way. The young Indian goes to the camp and sings songs. They were great singers. Another young Indian would come with his songs next night, until the seventh one comes. On the seventh night, she selects the one who will be her man. Then she is asked which of the singers she liked best. She says which she liked, and that is her man. Some have love songs. Others have warrior songs, wild bird songs, hunting songs, or great spirit songs. A love song tells what he will do when she gets in his canoe and paddles away. If she takes a liking to that, then he's her man. When she selects her man, she sings back, and then it's all over. It is pronounced by the chief medicine man when the great marriage feast will take place.

Another way is the best hunter. The old folks go to the girl's home.

They don't take their son, but they tell of their boy having great luck trapping beaver, bears, otter, and birds. The old woman who has the daughter says to her, "How do you like that story?" Well, she likes the story about this great hunter. Next night they bring their son. They say, "Now here's my son. He had all that luck, and last night you said you liked that story about my son. Now here he is." This is the first time they've met.

The boy says, "I come here to see if you'll cook for me." Then if she says "Yes," all the neighborhood knows, and they say, "*Mattamalia!*" They all shout through the neighborhood, "*Mattamalia!*" It means "all willingness." Everyone cheers from one camp to another. "*Mattamalia!*" is a cheer.[2]

No conversation was allowed between the young people at any time. If you see two talking together, they must marry whether they like each other or not. No courtin' except only the above ways. I remember Fanny Bonus, Will Bonus's daughter, what lived at Springhill Junction, was seen talking to Louis Prosper thirty-five years ago. The old people said, "You've been seen talking to him; you must marry him."

She said, "I don't like him."

They said, "You've got to marry him."

She said, "If I marry him, I'll not live with him."

I was at the wedding. The same day of the wedding, she left on the train for Truro. I was on the same train. They have never lived together. This was thirty-five years ago. He is in Liverpool, Nova Scotia, and she is in New Brunswick. It's the parents' love. 'Taint the young ones'.

The Indian man is not supposed to marry before he is forty years old. A girl must marry much younger, before she is fifteen years old. She may be married at two years old, but then her parents keep her until she is nearly fifteen. The idea likely is that when a man gets old, he will have a young woman to help him. When he can no longer hunt, his squaw can hunt food.

If parents with a child two years old arrange with parents of another two-year-old for their children to marry, the chief medicine man will be called, and he will announce when the marriage will take place, say at fifteen years. This is the way some Indian men marry young. Fun is often poked at those married young: "Your young ones and yourself will all be same age."

Indian women are not supposed to marry twice. A widower may marry again, but a widow is not supposed to marry. They are left aside to take care of the young ones growing up. And wives don't like to be called after their husbands. They like to return to their own names. They don't like to get into white ways. Some Indian children grow up without knowing their mother's Christian names. The Indian father calls his wife *E'n*, and the mother calls the father *E'n* also.

> "*Ain!* My love!
> My husband!"
> A term of endearment
> uttered with an
> inclination of the
> body.
> — Silas Rand,
> *Micmac-English
> Dictionary*

Words for the Family

Nujj	my father
Nkij	my mother
Wijikitiek	my sibling
Nsis	my elder brother
Njiknam	my younger brother
Nmis	my elder sister
Nkwe'ji'j	my younger sister
Nklamuksis	my uncle
Nuji'j	my grandchild
Pitu'-nuji'j	my great-grand child
Njilj*	my father-in-law
Njukwi'jij?	my mother-in-law
Niskamij	my grandfather
Kji-pitu'-niskamij	great-great grandfather
Kkwis	your son
Ktus	your daughter
Kniskamij	your grandfather. That word now also means your stepfather. In those days there was no stepfathers.

The Camp Work

Indian women tell the girls, assembled in the camp for the purpose of getting instructed, how to treat their husbands, and how to be their servants all their lifetime. They tell them how, when he brings in animals, they must dress the small animals and how to cook certain parts of it. When he brings in birds, how they are to be cooked in a certain time. Then again the fish, how to serve them.

In many cases, they smoked the birds, meat, and fish for further use. Indians lived on animals and fish. The meat was bear, moose, caribou, and beaver. They smoked it. Fish were preserved and smoked also. When it is too hard to hunt, we have something to fall back on. Liver of each animal is used as bread.

Women must serve their husbands all their lives. They are told and bound down to that, and the chief medicine man is supposed to see this carried out. They musn't call their husband by his name, but just address him as *E'n*, and he will address her the same, *E'n*.

About the water. They have clay work and birchbark work and all that kind — for holding water. The women must get all the water for the camp use. Get the water in the evening. This water can be used in the evenings, and what is laid over, overnight, all them dishes has to be emptied out and fresh water brought before breakfast. They get up with the sun. My wife always gets up with the sun.

The dishes — well, what you put the meat on. It is sometimes served on a stick. One end is stuck in the ground. The other end is cut every time you use it. Sometimes the meat is served on a piece of birchbark. This birchbark is never used again, but it is put in the fire. This is not always done, but these are the directions the girls is given.

Near the mouth of Nine Mile River and Shubenacadie, at the Forks on the Halifax side, there are six or seven boulders of a funny shape. Seems as if these rocks were made for washing clothes. Indian women call them *etli-ksistaqte'kemk*, meaning, "in the process of washing clothes by pounding."

The Indians dipped their clothes in the river, put them on the stones, which had a hollow as if gouged out, and pounded them with sticks, ordinary sticks. This pounded the dirt out. They never used soap, but rubbed the clothes with hardwood ashes, rolled them up, dipped them in the water to let the ashes soak through, then pounded them on the rock with sticks. This pounded the dirt out and fetched the dirt out.

You get the hardwood ashes by burning hardwood. The lye of the ashes takes the dirt out, draws the dirt out, and bleaches it. Sprinkle ashes on the clothes, roll them clothes up, put them in the water, and let them lay for a few minutes. Repeat that four or five times on one piece. The lye works out and bleaches the clothes. Put them on the rock, pound them with a stick, and repeat. This sends the ashes through. Then rub them out in the water. Put them again in the water and rub them in your hands. Then they are all ready to bleach. Spread and pound them when rolled — not singly or it would tear the clothes.

No water where it has laid overnight is to be used in the morning. It must be poured out and fresh got. The woman does all that. Besides, she makes all her clothes and the moccasins for him and her to wear. She makes the snowshoes except the bows or rims. She fills in the bows with thongs. Then they are all ready for him to use.

The man's duty is to make his *tepaqn* — his hand-sled — and his bow and the arrows. Only the woman, she ties the feathers on the arrow and also ties on the arrowhead. She has nothing to do with making the arrowhead, only tying it on.

The woman always knows pretty well what time her man is coming from the hunting expedition. She gets everything ready, wood and water, and looks out for him. She goes and meets him as far as she can see him. Then she knows what luck he has had. She goes in camp first and tells the young ones while the man puts away the stuff outside. They are all glad when she breaks the news to the young ones. Then he goes in, and there is plenty of wood and water. Perhaps she has the meal ready — what he got the day before or sometime before that.

In the evening, or rather after supper, he goes out visiting and tells what he has seen or heard or what he got. When the woman knows where he is visiting, she tells the young ones, "You mustn't go into that camp while your father is there, unless I send you on an errand." If a friend comes to see him, then the woman sends one of the children to the camp where he is visiting to let him know. Otherwise they must not go.

The woman goes to work and picks up the animal bones carefully and puts them a good piece away from the camp. Fish bones or feathers she burns, but bones she hides away from the camp, as it is bad luck to fall over animal bones. She then lays away the wishbones from the birds, beavers, porcupines, or rabbits. The shoulder blade of the rabbit is the wish bone.

While the man is visiting, she pulls out one of the wishbones, a shoulder blade of a rabbit, and tells the children to wish. She makes the children put the bone on the fire coals and tells them to wish an animal for their father for tomorrow or for his next hunting trip. The bone burns, turns brown, and gives the shape of an animal or head. When the father returns from his visit, the woman tells him what luck he will have tomorrow, whether bird or animal or fish. She says, "You are going to kill a heron, a loon, a wild goose," or so on. They have all these forms to go through, and the woman teaches the children this as she was taught by the old women. In the porcupine, the wish bone is the shoulder blade. It has a hole in it, which represents a lake. In the beaver, the wishbone is the shoulder blade. It has a hole in it like the porcupine's.

The children sit around and make a wish. The child chosen to wish makes a hole with his thumb and first finger. He puts both arms above his head and tries to see which part of the hole he hits. This represents the part of the lake his father will visit. The lake is all surrounded with thick woods. If the child misses the hole, it means his father will miss the lake. If he hits it fair and square, his father will have good luck and hit the lake. If not, he will miss his way and will have to come back and start again. An Indian never gets lost. He can always find his way home, but he may miss a particular corner of the lake.

From the porcupine, another thing Indians get is quills for ornamenting quill boxes. Porcupine quills are very white, and Indians dye them different colours. Make them into boxes. Birchbark is cut from the tree in June when it strips easily. Middle of June is the time. Extra grains for tree are made then, and bark peels off easily. Bark is sewn with roots of young spruce. The roots are split and peeled, and we make a hole with an awl. Then the birchbark is pierced with an awl to place each quill in. Porcupine quillwork extends back two hundred years and is handed down. So is work with wood.

Black ash is used for baskets and white ash for axe handles. Black ash is pliable and springs too much, but it does for basket work. White ash does not give and does for axe handles and bows and arrows. Green wood does for that. Canoe paddles are made of different kinds of wood. Rock maple is the wood we use to make paddles for a man — an Indian man — because it is the hardest wood we have. Women's paddles are made of red spruce wood because it is lighter.

When they bury an Indian, his pipe is buried with him and his implements he thought most of are buried with him. Arrowheads are common. The body is sewn up in birchbark, and these articles are sewed up with him. The things the Indian loved.

I Am the Only Medicine Man in Nova Scotia

The chief medicine man's duty was to tell the great historical legends, to lecture on them and to unite couples, to marry them. He instructed couples after the marriage, where to go and what to do for the life to come. Tells them to lead a good life, and they and their children would be with Kluskap when he returns to take us north.

The medicine man chastises anyone who needs it, according to their deeds. The culprit is then turned over to the warrior chief, and he sets his warriors to tie him to a stake. Wood is gathered and piled around him and set fire to. He is burned alive or he is skinned alive according to his deed. If he has done something that does not merit death but still is a breaking of the law, he is whipped by the warrior chief with withies. They did not have jails or penitentiaries.

This did not happen very often, as the Indians were pretty good. It is about four hundred years since the last punishment was given to Indians here, or since we came under British and French laws. If children were disobedient, the matter was reported to the medicine man, and they were turned over to the warrior chief to be whipped. Parents never whipped their children themselves. If they were found whipping them, they were whipped themselves, so there was no chance of cruelty by parents.

Mi'kmaw chiefs and captains with their families, Pictou, 1923. Jerry Lonecloud stands in the centre of the back row; his wife, Elizabeth Paul, is at extreme right. (NSM, N-10,523)

If their limbs are broken or they get any kind of diseases, they go to the chief medicine man, and he has all kinds of wild medicines. He sets bones and doctors them for sickness. The chief medicine man of a tribe is supposed to know about all the wild plants, how to gather them, and what to give when affliction comes.

Medicinal Plants[3]

The following chart and text contain Lonecloud's remedies and tonics made from plant and animal parts. Please DO NOT experiment with these. Some are highly toxic and can cause death. For treatment of illness, consult your physician.

I have gathered all of these in Nova Scotia, except the wild onion, and many others that I know to see but do not remember.

Princess pine [*Chimaphila umbellata*, var. *cisatlantica*]

Rock polypody or golden fern [*Polypodium virginianum*]

Sasparas [Sarsaparilla, *Aralia nudicaulis*] Herbs come both in soft and
    hardwood, like sarsaparilla.

Snakewood, not ginger [unknown; Rand's *Micmac English Dictionary*
    has *tcegawobe*, snake root, sarsaparilla]

Bloodroot [*Sanguinaria canadensis*]

Spikenard [American Spikenard, *Aralia racemosa*]

Ground ivory, called squaw vine [unknown]

Skunk cabbage root [*Symplocorpus foetidus*]

Wild Indian turnip [Jack-in-the-pulpit, *Arisaema triphyllum*]

Wild onion [*Allium tricoccum*]

Black cherry bark [*Prunus serotina*]

Red cherry bark [*Prunus*, possibly *virginiana* or *pennsylvanica*]

Bayberry leaves [*Myrica pennsylvanica*]

Black raspberry roots [*Rubus* spp.]

Blackberry roots [*Rubus* spp.]

Indian cup or lady's slipper [possibly pitcher plant, *Sarracenia*
    purpurea]

Indian chocolate [*Geum rivale*] Great medicine, a herb not very
    tall, makes a chocolate drink, grows in swampy places. Leaves,
    three or four inches across, generally three leaves to a stalk.
    Grows along the ground.

Blackroot [unknown] Great medicine to kill worms: tapeworms, pinworms, stomach worms. It is also medicine for the eye. It grows flat on the ground, something like strawberries.

Witch-hazel [*Hamamelis virginiana*]

Moosewood [*Acer pennsylvanica*]

Black ash bark [*Fraxinus nigra*] Used for worms.

Sweet fern [*Comptonia peregrina*, or *Myrica peregrina*]

Elm bark [*Ulmus americana*]

Ground hemlock [*Taxus canadensis*] Grows two feet above the ground, not very tall.

Ground juniper berries [*Juniperus communis*]

White hellebore [*Veratrum viride*] Grows in New Brunswick.

Solomon's seal [*Polygonatum pubescens*] Has beautiful strings of red berries, nice.

Snake head [*Chelone glabra*] Has a white flower like a snake's head, and eyes are there, mouth and tongue. Just perfect as it was made.

Wild rose [*Rosa* spp.] Good for diabetes.

Bakeapple [*Rubus chamaemorus*] You find it in Kentville, Blue Mountain, and other parts of Nova Scotia. It grows on a vine like a cranberry. Good for kidney trouble. Right name of bakeapple is Bear-Vine apples. Bears eat the blossoms.

Indian hemp [*Apocynum cannabinum*]

Dogwood [*Cornus* spp.]

Frogwood [unknown] Grows on a bush.

Water pepper [*Polygonum hydropiperoides*] Has little green leaves and grows on bottoms of brooks. Very hot. Good for cold or cough.

Lobelia [*Lobelia inflata*] Indian tobacco.

Disease. When the Lord put disease on earth, he put medicine, and he put man to locate medicine. It is handed down like traditions. I am the only medicine man in Nova Scotia. At the St. Anne's Day mission, there were three chiefs. They looked to me for medicine. I have cured fits, asthma. I treats miners what get choked with dust. One tells another. I have many testimonials of people I cured from flu. People's mouths is my best testimonials.

FOR COLDS: bayberry root. One teaspoon in cup, then put in boiling water. Make five doses out of a cupful. Cures colds overnight.

FOR INDIGESTION: squaw vine, black cherry bark, blackwood, dogwood, princess pine, wild red cherry bark, teaberry leaves, and mountain tea vine. Mountain tea vine takes gas off stomach.

OILS AND GALLS: Use bear galls. Put alcohol in a bottle with it. One teaspoon of gall with hop bitters. One wineglass of bitters with gall in it. Beaver gall for rheumatism. Skunk oil for rheumatism and stiff joints. Coon oil for rheumatism and stiff joints. Wildcat oil for rheumatism and stiff joints. Big-horned owl — cat owl with ears like cat — oil for rheumatism. Bear oil for rheumatism.

FOR FEVER SORES: Use spruce partridge's liver, sliced and put on, or crow or raven's liver, sliced and put on. Cures it. Or them big cranberries, mash them up. Put on raw between layers of rag.

FOR FITS: Use oyster shells. Bake the shells over a fire. When thoroughly burnt, they'll fry. What is left, put in hot water, set off, and let cool. Take liquor off to one-half cup. Dose is one wineglass full, two or three times a day until half a gallon is used. This will cure any hard case of fits. I used to cure fits. I cured many cases in Halifax.

FOR CONVULSIONS in infants, take porcupine quills, burn them, put them in a dish, pour on cold water, and set away until dissolved. For a baby with convulsions, scrape a mud turtle's tail, and treat same as porcupine quills.

The tail must be dried. Or scrape caribou's horn, cured, then burn same as porcupine quills. Put in water. Give freely, same as water. For infants with convulsions, burn feathers of partridge, wild goose, or wild duck. Same as porcupine quills. Get a flat stone, heat it, and put feathers on. Porcupine quills can be put in the fire.

Indians used THISTLE, BAYBERRY ROOT, and ASH. The bark and the root is burnt for cancer. An equal measure of each. Common field thistle root, burn it and pound it. Burn black ash. Ashes of bayberry root are ground fine, burnt, and pounded fine. Put as a plaster on the cancer. It draws it out. Very painful.

WHITE AMERICAN HELLEBORE is poison. The root is found on the Kennebecasis River. I use it for cancer. It was brought here by American refugees from New England. I dreamed of a cure for cancer.

INDIAN CUP ROOTS were used by Dr. Paddy Lane in his cure for smallpox.[4]

All this was done before doctors were thought of. Cases were nearly always successful.

Disease. Bad spirit gives you disease. Indians believed greatly in prevention. Indians make medicine and go through a ceremony with the medicine to drive out the evil spirit before they take it, so the evil spirit can't leave any sting upon the body. Sick or well, the medicine is taken two times a year. Spring and fall, everyone took it.

When medicine is gathered in summer and winter, it is put aside, and a dance takes place in winter. Medicine man gets up a dance to thank Kluskap for the privilege of having medicine put away for the season and to ask for his cure with the medicine. Medicine man leads off and dances until he is exhausted. Then he pronounces all medicine gathered good. This lasts sometimes seven hours. If the medicine man can dance a certain length of time, the medicine is good. If not, it will be bad. Medicine was made in secret. They danced around it. A ceremony the evil spirit doesn't like is performed so he can't get in them. This, of course, is on the superstitious side.

THE NIGHT MEDICINE is *meteteskewey*, "the tapping one," and is the most mighty medicine — only one herb. Sometimes in the woods you hear water dripping on the leaves, like a ticking. This is the noise it makes. It has two large leaves. The Night Medicine can only be found at night. Andrew Abram of Truro found it He heard the drip, the tap. This is the way you are guided to it. He said it had a long stalk, ten inches to twenty-four inches tall, with long leaves, but only two leaves. Abram was supposed to leave a quarter of the roots, so he wouldn't offend the Great Spirit. But he took it all home. His wife said, "It will never cure because you have taken it all."

Joseph Howe Jeremy, son of John Jeremy of Kejimkujik, was named after Premier Joseph Howe. In later life, he dropped the name Jeremy, and Howe remains the surname of his descendants.

It is always in a thicket. It is very bashful. It hides. You always approach it backwards, guided by the drip. This medicine is the Great Spirit's cure and is said to cure anything you say to cure. When an Indian gets the One Medicine, he can cure anything, he thinks. Meteteskewey is the most mighty medicine and is only one herb. It is now known to only one or two. Joe Howe, aged eighty-odd, of Elmsdale, who lives in the first shanty after crossing Elmsdale bridge, knows about it. Those who used it among themselves are dead and gone.

KJI-NPISUN, the Great Medicine, is the Seven Compounds medicine. It has seven ingredients: princess pine; Indian cup root; sarsaparilla; ground hemlock; wild red cherry bark; black cherry bark; wild parsnip. Kji-npisun is made in compound for any disease — fever or wounds, rheumatics, apoplexy, anything. No particular dose. They can have all they want to drink. It will cure insanity. It is a herb compound for seven different diseases: erysipelas, neuralgia, stomach trouble, kidney trouble, liver trouble, scrofula, and rheumatism. It will help fits and strokes when other bark is added, and still another bark for fits.

So Here's What I Remember

I came back to Mother's old homestead at St. Margaret's Bay and stayed around about Halifax and down east Guysborough County and all them places.

Thirty-two years ago, I did this for a show. The Geldert brothers, two brothers weighing two hundred and forty and two hundred and thirty-six pounds respectively, took hold of my hair. I had hair to my waist. I braided my hair, and I swung them two men around by my braids. They was hanging on my braids, my hair was so healthy. I sold hair tonic. Both of them was ship's captains, from around Lunenburg.

At Sheet Harbour, Tangier, Clam Harbour, Jeddore, Musquodoboit Harbour — three times — I'd swing the two heaviest men there. Three times at Meagher's, Cobalt, and Stewart's. I lectured on customs and habits of our race. In school houses at these places, I lectured and performed on the strength of my hair tonic. I lived at Liscomb Mills eighteen years.

My chief work is to get the herbs and make medicine. I could furnish testimonies for every day in the year of cures I done. I'm always hunting various kinds of animals and birds. I'm a crack shot. A great guide. I been going about Halifax and Liscomb now for thirty-three years. Had a medicine show first, but I found Nova Scotia a good hunting ground and settled down. Been back around Halifax 'bout ten years.

I lecture on Indian legends and customs and habits of Indians. Hunting and fishing and medicine. When I was a boy, the chief medicine man would gather the children, boys and girls, into his camp and tell them stories. In those days, they had a council wigwam, where they held all their sayings and doings, and it was in this council room these legends were told. Some old people would be there also, listening judges, like — to see if he told them correctly. Every word has to be put in its proper place.

People there knows the stories as good as him, but they're not to be told by them, only by the chief medicine man. There's not supposed to be one word out of the way, same as scripture. Oftentimes, by making mistakes, they might lose their chiefship. Then they would be put away and a new chief elected. It is not very often this occurs, but this is what happened when it did occur.

I heard these stories over sixty years ago and also since in the camps. Heard them at Point Levi when I was twenty. Different medicine men told them in their different tribal languages. Stories told in those long nights — all the stories we used.

This is how I learned these stories. Stories without end.

Jerry Lonecloud posing at Climo Studios, Halifax, with a knife made of moose bone. (NSM, N-1663)

THREE
Stories Without End

These are the a'tukwaqn stories, passed down by generations of Mi'kmaw elders. Lonecloud heard versions of them from the time he was born. Reading these tales is hearing the elders speaking through the ages, yet their words are filtered through the times and the experience of one particular man — Jerry Lonecloud.

When Lonecloud recounted legends to Clara Dennis, he tried to fit Mi'kmaw stories, first told to him as a child in the 1850s and 1860s, into a shape that conformed with what he afterwards learned of the world. In telling the story of Sinmaju and the flood, for example, he introduces the Rocky Mountains into a Mi'kmaw tale usually told about the formation of Prince Edward Island. He also struggled to interpret these stories in light of modern science, to enable Dennis to understand them. He knew she had no knowledge of Mi'kmaw worldview, in which all animate beings are shape-changers and take many forms at will. The Mi'kmaw cosmos saw animacy, actual persons, in mountains, lakes, winds, seasons, or directions, and in many other things which western science definitely did not consider alive.

Mi'kmaw stories of these persons show them in varying guises, sometimes living as humans or resting as mountains, sometimes taking many different shapes within a single story. Lonecloud dealt with this cultural difference simply by telling Dennis, "Kluskap changed them." But Lonecloud also knew animal behaviour and Mi'kmaw landscapes, the stars in the night sky, the seasons and weather, from years spent in the woods. Often he slips seamlessly from telling the tales into connecting them to his own keen observations of these things, which were such a large part of his own life.

In this, he is following a Mi'kmaw tradition thousands of years old, using the multiple layers of meaning in stories to pass on hard-won experience and observations, his own and those of the people, the sa'qwe'ji'jk, before him.

Under the surface layer of such stories, underlined by their comedy and tragedy, lies a wealth of information about animal behaviour, the location of resources, hunting techniques, or instructions on how to behave well. The one central driving mission of the a'tukwaqn is to teach: to teach survival in a fluid, dangerous, and beautiful world.   R.H.W.

The Origin of Man

Here's about the origin of man. How we come here.

Kji-kinap was first. He made everything, and then he took a rest and lay on the ground to see what he had done. He found a stone image like a person, and it looked so perfect. He found a stone image that was like a person. He come up to it, and it looked so like a man he spoke to it and asked, "What are you doing here?" No response. Asked the second time and no response. Third time he stooped and blew his breath in the image's mouth. The image came to.

Adam made out of mud, not so good. Stone is better.

Kji-kinap said, "What are you doing here?" But the image did not answer. He said the same thing three times, then stooped down and blew his breath into its nostrils. The stone came alive like a person. Kji-kinap said, "Sit up, stand up!" and the image walked. Then he said, "I'm going to name you. Your name is Kluskap. *Kluskap* in our language means, "You will be doubted in all your sayings and doings. They'll doubt your words whatever you do." It is an odd name, but there is no other name besides.

Kji-kinap was first. He was greater than Kluskap. Sun is great spirit, Kluskap is the second spirit. Kji-kinap is the great spirit of all who made the earth and all therein. Kluskap was left alone after the creation. The other two spirits, the Sun and Kji-kinap, went away. We believe this. These legends belong to an age this side of Kluskap. These is stories told correctly, no hearsay, stories told correctly by chiefs and handed down by generations.

The great spirit is Kluskap. Greater than the great spirit is Kji-kinap. Kji-kinap said, "Sit up!" and Kluskap sat up. "Stand!" and he stood up.

"Walk!" and he walked. "Stop!" and he stopped. He named him Kluskap. Kji-kinap says to Kluskap, " I have not finished this place. There is a lot of riley water." He wanted the water clean for fish.

Kji-kinap, "great power."

"Clear the brooks of rock, and make a passage for the water to the sea. When you go to do that, you will see a serpent on the other side of the river. He will speak to you. The serpent will say to you, 'Kluskap, What are you doing here?'"

Kluskap. A bird behind Kluskap's shoulder said, "Fire and kill the serpent." He struck the serpent in the head. The serpent was bleeding freely. The bird was a woodpecker, a large bird.

Kluskap said, "You have done well, and I am going to put something on you that you will always carry to the end of the world. He scooped two handfuls of blood of the serpent, put them on the bird's head, and called him Black Woodpecker, *An'tawe'j.* The bird has a scarlet head to this day. Woodpecker was then the only bird in the world. Kluskap. The Great Black English Woodpecker belongs to the Kluskap age.

After Kluskap did his day's work — he worked by the day — he went to his wigwam.

Before sundown, he noticed a young girl coming along the path where he had come from after his day's work. She came to the front of the wigwam and stood there.

Kluskap asked her, "What are you doing here?"

"I am come to help you. I am smart. I am young."

She said she was sixteen years old. She remained. The next day Kluskap finished up his work. Kinap made the trees, but Kluskap and this girl finished the work. They made the leaves. To the girl Kluscap said, "Here's trees, but no leaves nor flowers nor birds. I want you to put leaves on trees, and on hackmatack to put needles. Burrs also, put on the trees." The seeds were in this. She put flowers on the shrubs underneath the trees all through the forest.

Kluskap said, "On these trees there will be birds who will sing for you."

To the girl, he said, "You said you were smart. We want birds. Birds in the trees." The birds were originally stars in the sky. The girl ordered her

Annie Gloade and Jerry Lonecloud, photographed by Climo Studios, Halifax, in 1927. Annie is modelling a costume from the Provincial Museum's collection. (NSARM, N-4179)

pet birds to come down where she was. She ordered Kulu, the Great Eagle, to bring them down to her after she put leaves and burrs on trees and flowers on low shrubs. Birds have the same names as stars because birds came from the sky.

A very red star seen after ten o'clock is the Robin, *Jipjawej,* so-called from its red breast. Wild Goose is *Sinumkw.* Brant is *Mokalawi'j,* nearly as large as Wild Goose. Old Squaw Duck is *Ka'qawikej.* Mother Carey's Chicken is *Mekopejuji'ej.*

"I have left my pets in heaven," the girl said, "and if there is any way to get them, I'll be glad." Kluskap furnished an eagle called Kulu. Kulu bought down

Clara Dennis adds this extract from the *Halifax Evening Mail,* dated "28 March or so": "Lonecloud, the well-known Indian doctor of Liscomb Mills, brought to the city the largest specimen of woodpecker ever seen in Nova Scotia. The bird measured twenty-nine inches from tip to tip of wing and eighteen inches from bill to tail."

ducks, eagles, crows, and all. Birds sang in trees, and loons made their noise, and ducks swam in lakes. The fish hawk, *Makwis,* went back to the sky. The other stars fished him up and took him up, and it was understood that they wanted the fish hawk's feathers. We notice this off and on when we see the bird rising until it goes out of sight.

At end of the second day's work, a young man came up the same path as the girl to the wigwam. Kluskap said, "Come in. What are you doing here?"

"I am come to help you. I am smart. I am seventeen years old."

Kluskap asked him what he didn't ask the girl: "Where did you come from?" Bishops and others have various theories as to our origin. They say we came from places like China or the Bering Strait. But we know where we come from — the sky. The young man answered, "I come from the sky." He broke the news where we come from. *Our* forefathers come from the sky. Adam and Eve come from the earth. So the Indians all come from the sky, and we always believed that we come this way into civilization, as you call it.

To the young man, Kluskap said, "You said you were smart and young. We want animals." This is 'bout the origin of animals. To the young man, he said, "We want animals."

Ajalquj,
"a hole, a den."
Silas Rand's *Micmac-English Dictionary*
defines *Ajalkutc* as
"the Pleiades, the
Seven Sisters."

The young man said, "I will use the same bird." He sent Kulu back to heaven, and he brought down the animals. They multiplied and went over the earth. The young man was sent to get the animals. The stars are named after every animal we have. Kulu or the Great Eagle brought them. Every animal we have in Nova Scotia has a star named after him.

Bear is Seven Stars, and there was Moose, Deer, Beaver, Mink, Otter. The animals were named up in the sky, and when the young man sent Kulu up, he named them all to Kulu and said, "Bring those down." And Kulu brought them all down, and they became animals of the earth. So the animals were originally stars, and when they came to the earth, they were animals. The young man named them, but they were originally stars in the sky.

The work the young girl and the young man did suited Kluskap. He said, " I am going to marry you together, and you will have children and they will have children." Kluskap took them out of his wigwam and married them. The ceremony has been lost for four hundred years. What words were said or what the ceremony was we don't know.

Kluskap said, "You claim you're so smart, and you've showed some of it here. Go and make your wigwam and live, and you'll have children and they'll have children. The man can go out in the forest and get the animals, and the woman can cook them." This was already known to them. Kji-kinap must have sent them down. They helped to finish the world. The woman finished the birds and trees, and the man, the animals.

The Seven Stars are known by the Indians as the Bear's Den. *Ajalquj* means Seven Stars, the Bear having come to earth at the call of the young man to his pets. I remember Indians pointing out the Bear's Den and those stars and others. There are two stars always the same distance apart. Both are named *Tahdahgoo,** both called by the one name. Gannet Bird is the star that comes out before daylight. Morning Star is *Ktatapn.* Morning Star was the last star made. North Star is an old man, *Kisiku-kloqoej.* He seldom blinks. Orion is three stars in a row, supposed to be three chiefs fishing together. Each has a line consisting of a row of stars. Three stars in a row. Each has a line of stars from it.

Our forefathers were stars. When they came upon earth, the woman star, she had birds, pets which she dearly loved. She did not want to leave them up with the other stars, and she couldn't get back up there again. So she made a vow to remain on earth forever. She called down her pets, the birds.

All these were stars, but the young girl and the young man called them down, and they remained on earth with their master and mistress.

Birds and Animals

These were all stars in her days, and she called them down.

Fish hawk	*Makwis*, scapegrace, a bird large as a loon
Partridge	*Plawej*
Spruce partridge	*Wijik*
Kingfisher	*Jukutali'kej*
Swallow	*Pukwales*
Chimney swallow	*Kaqtukwaqnji'j*. Thunder Bird in our language. When you see this bird around, it is a sure sign of thunder.
King bird	*Deardardeoalie**, means "shaking his wings fast." He's king of all birds. All the birds fear this bird, even the eagle, whom he taps on the head with his sharp beak.
Teal	*Wissadaej** means small size blue wing duck.
Brown thrush	*Glowgleetch**
Brown sparrow	*Cahscalegenetch**
Thrush	*Mali'si'skwe'j*, named after his song, which sounds like the word *mali'si'skwe'j*, "Maliseet girl."
Bittern	*Mooreeawdom**, belongs to the crane family.
Heron	*Tmkwaliknej*

White eagle	*Kitpu*
Fish hawk	*Wisow-makwis (-kuk)*
Gannet	*Tahgahgoo**, *Tahdahgoo**
Gull	*Kloqntiej*
Blue wing duck	*Apji'jkmuj*
Shell bird	*Tmaqni'j*, Pipe Bird
Mackerel gull	*Neektoolnetch**
Nighthawk	*Pi'jkwej* [also a nickname for Beatrice]
Blue Jay	*Tities*, pretty name and pretty bird
Whippoorwill	*Wi'kkwili'tej*
Black English woodpecker	*An'tawe'j*
Crow	*Ka'kaquj*
Raven	*Kji-ka'kaquj*
Robin	*Jipjawej*
Goshawk	*Pipukwes*
Loon	*Kwimu*
Chickadee	*Chickéégetch**
Brown wren	*Nomatháló0**
Golden warbler	*Watapji'jit*, "little yellow one"
Red warbler	*Puklawji'jit*
Linnet	*Mekweji'jit*, "little red one"
Grosbeak	*Kinisquatji'jit*, "little proud one, or sharp head, or crested head"
Snipe	*Jijwikate'j*
Woodcock	*Wnaqpitiesiku*, "little one uplifting, raising one's voice"
Hummingbird	*Militaw,* "all over the place"
Bumblebee	*Amu* [from *mijipjamuej*]
Yellow wasp	*Amuej*
Black hornet	*Maqtewe'j*, "the black one," probably not the real name

The man was lonely for his animals, and he called them down.

Moose	*Tia'm*
Caribou	*Qalipu*
Bear	*Muin*
Lucifer	*Apuksikn* (cat family)
Marten	*Apistane'wj*
Wildcat	*Qajue'wj*
Otter	*Kiunik*
Beaver	*Kopit*
Muskrat	*Ki'kwesu*
Fisher cat	*Pkmk*
Weasel	*Iskus*
Mouse	*Apukji'j*
Deer	*Lentuk*
Wolverine	*Ki'kwa'ju*
Walrus	*Pastiko'pijit*
Sea Seal	*Hahcheyoh**
Seal	*Waspu*
Polar bear	*Muinuapsk*
Fox	*Wowkwis*
Flying squirrel	*Soxcohdoo**
Red squirrel	*Apalpaqmej*
Striped squirrel	*Atu'tuej*
Rabbit	*Apli'kmuj*
Porcupine	*Matues*
Skunk	*Apukjilu*
Racoon	*Amaljikwej*
Woodchuck	*Munumkwej*

Kluskap performed great miracles, handed down generation upon generation.

Kluskap said, "Time coming when people will come on the hunting ground and take the land from you, but I go north and will prepare you a hunting ground. You can't come there until after your death. You got to die here."

We never knew Christ was crucified until they told us. We never heard of it. The white man put great fear into the Indian. He thought the end of the world would come, for it had been prophesied that the white man would come and take the land before the end of the world. Kluskap said, "There will be white people come and take your land from you. But I go to make you a happy hunting ground. There shall be no other nation enter it, and there shall be no one to molest you. If you are wicked, there is a place of darkness forever — no sun there. Indian will have to hunt his game in the dark. The bad Indians are going to be left in the dark, where there will be no sun. Dark place for their hunting ground. Couldn't see game flock."

Kluskap went north and visited all the tribes in British North America. He promised he would come back. He said, "And you shall all rise from the ground, from the branches, from the crutches of the trees, and from the scaffolds."

The old Indians used to bury their dead in the crutch of the trees and also on scaffolds seven or eight feet high. They'd put the body on top of scaffolds, and they were devoured by eagles or fowls of the air. "But I'll come and rise you from the mounds of the earth, and I'll call you down from the trees."

Kluskap made a promise he would come back at the end of time. Still I cling to the old same thing. I call it, God will come.

Kluskap also prophesied that no live Indian would see the end of the world. Indian chiefs said, "When we tell these stories about Kluskap, the end of the world is at hand. These things were prophesied. When these are known to the white people, the end of the world is to come."

You is the first time a white person has ever heard this story.

Sinmaju and the Flood

Sinmaju was a great man and a great lover of birds, animals, and people. He prophesied that all the mountains would be under water. People did not believe him. He blew a whistle in one of the great lakes, and bubbles came up. They froze and formed an iceberg. Well, two-thirds of this iceberg was submerged, and birds, animals, and Indians stayed on top and made caves. Sinmaju got moss and food for different birds and animals. When he got all the food for his family, the rains came. The iceberg tossed about and finally grounded in the Rocky Mountains. Stuck there. Water began to fall, and she cantered over into the valley and spilled out animals and birds and Indians. All not in this iceberg perished.

Kukwesk, the cannibals, were destroyed. The *Wikulatmu'jk*[1] didn't get on the iceberg. They said they would stay. They wanted to keep their word. They said, "You go." They thought the Indians were going to a different world, and they said, "We will stay here. The white man will take your land." All the rest of the noble race of Indians were destroyed by the flood.

After the flood, Sinmaju sent birds to see if there was any land. Sinmaju sent out birds and said, "Go and see where we are." Birds understood Sinmaju. They had the same language. Sinmaju sent the Raven out. The Raven was white. Whitest bird, he was white as snow, white as mountains. The Raven did not return. Raven is same family as the Crow, only a bigger bird.

At the time of the flood, the Crow was as white as a gull. He was sent out to discover land. The Crow and the Raven were sent out by Sinmaju. The Crow heard that the Raven had good luck, and the Moosebird was telling the Crow what good luck the Raven had. The Moosebird said in the bird language three times, "Some bird had bad luck, but still it come round good luck for all." The Moosebird was singing it, and the Crow was astonished. The Crow said, "Caw caw!" The Indians use this expression when they are astonished.

The Meatjay was singing, "Those that had bad luck have good luck for all." The Crow and Raven were feasting on the dead bodies. Meatjay or Moosebird told on them.

Mi'kmaw re-enactors photographed in 1923 during the celebration of the landing of the first Scottish settlers in Pictou from the ship Hector *in 1783. Jerry Lonecloud is the third man from the left in the front row, and he is holding his moose-bone knife straight up.* (NSM, N-12,170)

Next Sinmaju sent this Weather Petrel, stormy petrel, a pretty bird, dark grey with a very white breast and under wings. And Mother Cary's Chickens, like a small pigeon. He is *Mekopeju* — has a narrow red rim around the lids of his eyes. He skims the water and feeds on scum of the water. A small bird, he is. He scans the ocean as he flies. The Weather Petrel brought in a bit of twig.

Then he sent a Wild Pigeon, blue slate colour, very pretty bird, a very fast flyer. He also brought in a twig to Sinmaju. Sinmaju was overjoyed and said, "There must be land where he got this."

After all this, he sent out the Eagle, the biggest bird he had, to bring back the two first birds he had sent out, the Raven and the Crow. The Eagle found them eating carcasses of animal and human flesh. The Eagle told on them when he found them. So Kluskap took the Raven, one of the prettiest birds of all, and said, "Since you did not return, you will be black." He told the Crow the same thing. And they have been black ever since.

Elizabeth Paul at the Hector Celebration, Pictou, 1923. She is seated, far left, in the row of Mi'kmaw women. (NSM, N-12,172)

To Mother Cary's Chickens, he said, "You have done so well and brought the news of land. You shall nest in twigs and bring up your young." To Pigeons, he said, "You will nest in trees and bring up your young." I often look at a nest, and it is always pieces of twig, and you can see the eggs through it, but still they rear the young that way.

Sinmaju settled, and he said, "Strange birds will come to me, and they will teach me words outside our language."

Sinmaju stayed where the iceberg grounded. He said to the people, "Go up there, and you will meet strange birds and fish, but there will be no kukwesk, no cannibals." The first man after the flood went north. Then one east and one south. When Sinmaju sent one family north to seek a river, they was to meet animals and birds and name them according to their habits and plumage. "You will have through them a different language," said Sinmaju.

He sent people east and said, "Also you will have a different language, and it will be learned of by the songs of your birds." To the one from the south he said, "You will have a different language, and the first generation will learn a good many words from the birds' songs and sayings." Their songs and talk distinguish the different birds. The three Indians would meet birds who would teach them a different language. Before the flood, all people spoke the same language.

Four men and their families. Sinmaju sent one north. He said, "You will come to a river. Go up it and inhabit it." He sent another east and one west. He said, "I will stay here where the iceberg cantered over and melted." But all that iceberg did not melt and is still on mountains to this day. Indians still believe that the everlasting snows of the Rockies came this way. Younger Indians are getting educated, but old ones still believe this.

White people say we come across the Bering Strait, from Japan, China, or some other nation, but we have legends. We always been here since the creation. We know we got rescued on an iceberg. On an iceberg, same as Noah. Great Spirit, he told the tribes there that the Rockies would be under water. Indians could not believe it. So Sinmaju come down to his own family. He formed this mountain of ice out of one of the lakes. He blew a whistle, and bubbles came up, froze, and formed crevices in an ice mountain. One third rose; two thirds sank. Birds and animals were rescued in it. Sinmaju provided for his family and animals. He said, "I will remain here because I am not going to last many years more."

When Cannibals Were Among Us

Cannibals. Kukwesk. Cannibals were destroyed the time of the flood. Sinmaju wouldn't have them. None were seen since, so the legend must be true. Sinmaju called everyone together at Lake Superior. He told them the world was to be destroyed by a flood. Pointing to the Rocky Mountains, he said they would be covered. This was too much for the cliff-dwellers and the cannibals. They jumped in their canoes and went away and were destroyed.

Before the flood, cannibals were here among us, and us Indians could understand them and them us. Howsomever, the old Cannibal had a son, and he married one of the Mi'kmaw Indians' women. First he kidnapped her. He brought her home in a birchbark pouch. In the pouch, he caught a little girl, a boy, and this Indian woman. The way he caught them, he used the birchbark pouch with a stick. He beat the birchbark pouch with a stick, and the noise was like a partridge drumming on a log. The little Indian boy went with his bow and arrows to shoot the partridge, and the little girl followed on to see how it was done. When he came handy to the noise, he found out it was the Cannibal. The Cannibal chased them, caught both of them, and put them in the birchbark pouch.

The woman was alone in the camp. She missed the children and went to look for them. While she was looking around, this Cannibal saw her and caught her and put her in the pouch and went home with all three of them. The Cannibal had only a father with him at home.

He said to his father, "I've got something to eat for you. I'll have one, you'll have the other one, and the big one we'll save to keep camp for us." They killed the two young ones, and they both ate one apiece. Roasted them on sticks.

Well then, it would be some time before the Cannibal started to hunt again. He would go different places and mostly bring back game or people — Indians — as animals were very scarce those times. He kept this up for years, until he and the woman had a child, a boy. The old man, he liked this grandchild of his.

Well now, he went back to this place where he caught the two children and the woman. He tried the same game once again — beat the birch pouch, imitated a partridge drumming. But the Indians said, "There's that there Cannibal back again. Now we must destroy him, kill him." So they all surrounded him, and they took with them some thongs — strings of moose hide — and twisted young yellow birch wood for withies. They caught him and tied him up with those thongs and the withies. Then they tied him to a tree, got plenty wood, and made a fire all around him until he was burned to death. Before he took fire, the Cannibal says, "I'll bring back the woman if you'll let me go back for her." But they would not, so he was burnt, and that was the end of him.

The old Cannibal, he was too old to go on a long hunting expedition, and he stayed round about home. He heard the Indians saying, "There's some more of those. We'll kill every Cannibal we come across and burn them up." Then he was obliged to stop at home, digging some roots what he could eat. He thought a good deal of the little grandson. He didn't want to eat him, but his intention was to kill the boy's mother and eat her — which he did.

One day while they were sitting all together in the camp, the old Cannibal, he pierced her with a wooden poker, poker for poking the fire, and killed her. Then he dissected her and told the little boy to take one part of the inside and put it into the well or spring. He told him not to hurry back, to play around. By the time he got back, the grandfather had et some of the boy's mother. The rest of it he put away for another time.

After a long while, he sent the boy to get some water, and when he got to the spring, before he dipped the water, he looked down in the bottom of the spring. There he saw a little boy, his brother. He beckoned to him to come up, and he did come up out of the spring. "Oh!" he says, "I'll come again. I have to take this water to our grandfather." Then every chance he'd get, he'd go and see his brother at the spring.

He grew very fast, this fellow in the spring. The first boy was always in a hurry to get back to his grandfather. This time the grandfather asked him, "What have you been doing?"

"Oh," he said, "I've been playing." It was not long before he had to get some more water for his grandfather. He liked this part very much, because he could see his brother and play with him. This time when he went to the spring, the little boy who was in the spring, he wanted to follow his brother. "Oh," he says, "You can't, for grandfather will kill you and eat you if you do. He killed our mother and et her, so best stay hidden." Then the second boy ran back to the spring and jumped in quickly out of sight.

The oldest cannibal boy went again to see his brother into the spring. Then they were playing round the woods round about the camp. Once in a while, the one who was in the spring, he says, "Did our grandfather kill our mother and eat her?"

The oldest one says, "Don't say that because Grandfather might hear you, and he don't know you're here."

The boy of the spring, he says, "Let's make a plan to kill our grandfather because he killed our mother."

The oldest one says, "I don't know that we can do that or not. Our grandfather is so big."

But the little boy of the spring, he says, "I've got a plan so we can kill him."

"Well, let's hear your plan."

"We'll peel some birchbark, plenty of it, and you go in with it into the camp, hang it around in the camp as an ornament." Which he did. And he stripped the bark, tied it into bunches, and got the camp all lined inside with the bunches.

When the Cannibal woke up, he says to the boy, "What are you doing with so much of this bark?"

"I'm just trimming inside this camp with the bark, so it will make it look nice."

So the old Cannibal says, "Oh, that's right, put some more wherever you think it is needed." Little boy of the spring, he had a lot of it gathered, and when the Cannibal went to sleep again, he just filled the camp with birchbark in bundles. Then he also he put big poles around the outside of the camp and placed big logs, what they could pick up, on the top and round the camp. So they sot fire to it, and they stood back and heard him screech. But he could not penetrate through the camp on account of the logs and flames and was actually burnt up.

Then they were left alone. They didn't know which way to go, but the oldest boy had always seen his father go the way the sun rises — towards the east. The oldest one, he says to the boy of the spring, "Now we got to leave here, and we don't know which way to go, which is the best way. But my father always went where the sun would rise. He'd go that direction." So they started on that journey.

They hadn't gone far before they heard some noise. They saw some children hollering, screeching, and playing. They made all kinds of noise. The two boys hung around them. They didn't want to approach right away. They didn't know who the children were. They thought they were the only two boys in the world. They didn't know of anybody else. They saw those little boys and girls playing around and heard the screeching. Those playing finally saw the two boys. Oh, they ran home to the camps and gave the alarm. They said, "We saw two persons in such a direction. We don't know what they were, who they were."

"Well," they said, "there's those cannibals around. Once there was one of them, now there are two." Then they surrounded them and captured them. Found out that they were the children of the woman who had belonged there, that they were only half-cannibal. Then found out how those cannibals et people. The oldest boy told what he saw when his father used to bring some children home in his pouch, and how he saw them roasted before the fire, and how his father et them. He told them how they burnt the old Cannibal to death. The oldest boy says, "I'll go and show you the place where the camp was, where we burnt this old Cannibal."

So the two boys went with a band of the Indians and found the camp and found the old Cannibal's bones burned white. Then the Indians went to work and pounded the bones to powder and threw them in the air. Then went back and took care of the boys. They married into the tribe and lost the cannibal part of them.

Kluskap and His Relations

This is about Kluskap when he was living with his relations. Time before he went away, although they did not know that he was going.

Now Kluskap had an uncle named Mikjikj. That's the word for a mud turtle. Kluskap's grandmother was *Kukumijnawainoq,* a toad. Kluskap's niece was named *Apistane'wj,* a marten or sable. The niece did the wigwam work, cooking and all. Kluskap's uncle was a great smoker and always liked to light Kluskap's pipe for him. Kluskap had his uncle for a servant also. In those days, Kluscap wore beadwork. He was the only one who had beaded clothes, clothes made from skins of wild animals.

One time they heard of a moose being near. It was wintertime, and many of the young men set out to chase the moose and kill it for the encampment where Kluskap was. Kluskap knew there were a great many young men on snowshoes. He said to his uncle, "I will loan you one of my snowshoes, and you go on the hunt, too. I will make you ready, but you can take only one of my snowshoes."

The uncle took the lead and made one step to their two, for he had only one snowshoe. He caught up to the moose and killed it and dressed it. Made a fire and roasted some part of it before the others overtook him. Mikjikj was warming his back to the fire. He says to them, "The fire is burning. You can roast some moose meat, too."

Now after a while Kluskap made his appearance with his other snowshoe. He said to his uncle, "Here is the tomahawk. You cut the limbs and little bushes to make a trail to where we shall carry our meat to the encampment." Mikjikj did so and completed the road. On his way out, he met the crowd again. Kluskap was ahead coming out. Mikjikj handed the pipe to Kluskap to take. Kluskap had another tomahawk, and he hit Mikjikj's hand and cut it off. His hand fell, and the pipe fell also. "Oh," said Kluskap, "that's your hand."

"Yes," Mikjikj said, "that's my hand. I was handing you a pipe. I didn't know you were going to cut my hand off." Kluskap picked up the hand and the pipe and stuck it on Mikjikj's hand again, and it was the same as before. The crowd that was with them saw that done. The hand was the same as before. Only the scar remained.

They came to the encampment with their moose, and it was taken to Kluskap's wigwam. There were a good many in the encampment. He got his uncle to deliver pieces of meat to every camp there. It looked as if the moose would not reach every one. Some knew, if Kluskap handed it out, they would all get a piece, and others doubted. But they all got a piece.

While Mikjikj was going around with the meat, he was told they were going to try and see who could jump the highest of the young Indians. The one who could jump the highest would have a great name and a prize. Mikjikj, when he came back from delivering the meat, told Kluskap there was going to be a great time jumping and a prize given.

Kluskap told his uncle, "I will lend you my *asueka'taqn coat.* Mikjikj was glad of this offer. He knew he would jump the highest. The jump was

Asueka'taqn,
"it wraps around."
An asueka'taqn was a
man's greatcoat without
buttons, worn wrapped
close and held by a
sash. Such greatcoats
replaced the blanket-
robe style of outer
covering in the
eighteenth century.

over the peaks of the wigwams. They began to jump, and Mikjikj's jump was way above the others. So he was supposed to get the prize. They all jumped over Kluskap's wigwam. Mikjikj, he says, "To make it interesting now, let us jump over the wigwam with our snowshoes on." So one of the young Indians of the encampment sailed over Kluskap's camp. Mikjikj put on his one snowshoe Kluskap had loaned him. He jumped over Kluskap's wig-wam. His snowshoe got caught on the wigwam pole. He could not get down.

Kluskap knew this was going on. He had just put on some green boughs in his fire, which made a terrible smoke where Mikjikj was at the top of the camp. Mikjikj said, "Don't put any more of those bushes on the fire. I'll get smoked up, and I can't get down from here." Kluskap sent out his niece to take him down. She took him down, but he did not get the prize for jumping so high.

Kluskap got news that he was wanted at a certain camp where there were two Indian girls. He told his uncle that he was wanted there to visit tonight. Kluskap said to his uncle, "I am not in the habit of going visiting, but I will lend you my *asueka'taqn*, and you'll go as me. I'll transform you into Kluskap." This was the only time Kluskap transformed anyone to himself. He transformed Mikjikj to himself. Mikjikj went that evening, and Kluskap remained at home.

When Mikjikj came to the wigwam where this family was, they were very delighted to see him, because they thought he was Kluskap come to pay them a visit, which was a great honour. But it was really Mikjikj. He abode with them two girls all night. All this time they thought they were treating Kluskap.

In the morning, he slept pretty late. Their breakfast was over, and they were wishing for him to wake up so they could serve him with his break-fast. It was getting so late they were getting out of patience. The woman of the camp, she thought she would peek, lift up the blanket by his head to see if he was awake or not. And as she lifted the blanket up, she saw

Mi'kmaq at Bear River about 1900. Jerry Lonecloud's sister, Sarah Michael, lived here after her marriage, and so did Jerry for a while. He is standing at right, wearing a black felt hat. (Glass negative by Harry Cochrane or Ralph N. Harris, collection of Danny Johnson; NSM, N-23,802)

Mikjikj. He was transformed immediately by Kluskap into a mikjikj, a mud turtle, for he had no business to stay all night with them two girls. This is the first time Kluskap transformed a man to an animal. Then Mikjikj stretched out, and the old woman says, "Where is Kluskap? I thought he was here all night."

The girls said, "No, he is there."

The woman of the camp says, "'Tain't Kluskap. It's a snake." Because his feet and head and body looked very queer. The woman of the camp, she took the stick used for poking the fire, lifted the blanket, and there was Mikjikj. She said to the people in the encampment, "What are we going to do with him?" Because he looked so horrible. They hadn't seen a turtle before, for this was the first time Kluskap had transformed a man to an animal. Kluskap punished his uncle Mikjikj in this way because he stayed all night.

The people says, "The way to do with him is to make a big fire, burn him up, and we'll get rid of the animal that way."

Mikjikj spoke then. He says, "That's just what I wanted, a fire, a good fire." When he was a man, he always liked a fire, a good fire, and would lay with his feet towards it.

"Oh," they said, "we knew that Mikjikj always liked a fire when he was a man, and this is how we can punish him." When they talked of making a fire, Mikjikj said they would be doing him good, as he always liked a fire when he was with Kluskap.

Then they said, "We can't kill him that way. We will cut a hole through the ice in the lake and throw him into that and keep him under there until he drowns."

Mikjikj thought that would be a good plan for him because he always liked to go into the water swimming very much. He did not tell them this time that they would favour him by throwing him in the water. When they gave out the word about cutting a hole in the ice and putting him in it, Mikjikj says, "Now here's where you're going to kill me. Every time I will poke up my head, they will knock it back again." All this time he was pleased with the plan they had to make away with him, for he knew he could live under water all winter. But he did not let them know that at the time. He made out he was much against the plan, and when they drug him out from the camp by each hind leg, every bush he could catch hold of, he would hang on every time. They would break his hold, and this went on until they got him to the lake.

When they got him to the lake, he tried to hold on to the ice, but his legs weren't strong enough. Still they drug him to the hole. When he got within one jump from the hole where they would put him in, he jumped in of his own accord. He was just waiting for the distance to come when he could jump. The last word he said when he made the plunge was "*Klu-damen!*"* Which means, " I can stay under water a long while."

After he said this, away he went and wintered in the lake and did not come up until next spring at the foot of the lake. It happened so that those two girls saw him when they went down to the river to do some washing, washing their clothes. They saw him swimming by. They knew him because he never changed any more. He had his shell on. When they saw him going by, they gave the alarm, saying they saw the same Mikjikj. When they gave the alarm, all wondered how Mikjikj could live under water all winter. The menfolks all went down to the water with spears and looked, but there was no sign of him. Only the girls saw him. He appears again in a period of time, but that is another story.

When Mikjikj was a man, he always tended the fire for Kluskap. Got the wood, made the fire and tended it, and laid beside it. Mikjikj did something wrong, but Kluskap let him off. He told a lie. On that occasion they had killed a moose, and the moose's heart was cooking. Kluskap's niece, the sable Apistane'wj, was helping. While she had her back turned, Mikjikj cut a slice off the heart and tasted it. He thought Kluskap wouldn't notice it.

When the household came in for their dinner, this heart was served on birchbark so it could be carved by Kluskap and divided up among them. Kluskap noticed there was a piece cut out of the heart, and he asked them, "Who cut a piece of the heart?"

There was only two in the camp cooking it, Apistane'wj and Mikjikj. Mikjikj spoke up and said, "I don't know."

He asked Apistane'wj, his niece. She did not know, of course, as she had her back turned when Mikjikj cut the meat. Then Kluskap never asked him no further questions. All this time Kluskap knew who it was. When he divided the heart among them, they all got equal shares except Mikjikj. When Kluskap came to Mikjikj, he gave him a very small piece because he had a piece before when it was cooking. He says, "This small piece is for you for telling me a lie. You had part of your share, now here's the other part."

The Marten, Kluskap's niece, was a great girl for play. Great with her bow and arrow and great for tobogganing. One day, she was coasting down with her toboggan, and she saw a porcupine. Porcupine is the slowest animal we have. "Oh," said she, "Grandmother, you better come and get aboard the toboggan, and I'll give you a coast." So they went coasting down a steep hill, and right ahead of them there was a cliff.

So the Porcupine said to the Marten, "Steer the toboggan straight. Don't hit any trees nor rocks." Her toboggan was heading for this cliff. The

Marten, she jumped out of the toboggan and let the Porcupine go on her own accord on the toboggan. The toboggan and Porcupine disappeared in the cliff out of sight. Got in some holes. The Porcupine has been living in the cliffs ever since and just goes out to feed. He eats bark and berries. Marten called her "Grandmother," but she wasn't, of course.

The Toad was very much respected by all the animals, and she was feared by the insects. She always kept her wigwam clean. She had a habit of sweeping all around the wigwam every morning, especially under the blueberry bushes. She kept them clean and would allow no insects to go up in the bush to disturb the flowers or the berries. When an insect would climb the blueberry bush, she would knock it down to the ground and kill it and then sweep it away.

The most troublesome insect was called the Blueberry Bug. He used to fly down to the blueberries, and she could not get that pest because every time she would go after him, he would fly to another bush. It were a bug, but it could fly, and she couldn't do anything with it. Blueberry Bug. Blueberry Bug has a scent like a peppermint, and when you are eating a blueberry and get him in your mouth, he tastes very strong like a peppermint and stings your mouth.

Kluskap thought a great deal of Toad, of her cleanliness. She kept everything clean. Kluskap informed the animals and birds to pay great respect to her all the time because he told them that this was his grandmother. Then she was busy all the time. She would go into the blueberry orchards, from one orchard to another, and when the insects heard her coming, they would mostly get out of her way because she would punish them so severely. When Kluskap got some meat, she always inspected the food. She was always a great inspector of food, to see there was no vermin or insects in it before it was served to Kluskap.

Her reward from Kluskap was that she was turned to a stone — Kuku-mijnawainoq, meaning "our Great-Grandmother." He threw a blanket over her shoulders and said, "You sit there until I come again." Kluskap's grandmother sits at Cape Split, looking out. Kluskap turned her into a stone to be remembered and seen by different tribes. He promised Grandmother that she should be turned to a person when he returned. So she looks in that direction ever since, expecting him to return. He'll come at the end of time.

We have Kukumijnawainoq in other places, too. English Mill Lake on Tusket Branch, that's the best one. That's a great one. She looks so alive in the face. You can see it miles away. Perfect. She is leaning towards the north, at the Narrows. Between the Narrows and Spar Lake, at the head of Tusket Forks. She's as high as this house. Has a shelf beside her, so she could put her hand down, a perfect shelf. This is a perfect one. She has a blanket over her shoulders, and a flat piece of rock, same as a shelf. You can go with a canoe and put the stuff on that shelf: meat, fish, punk, or tobacco for good luck, or even flint rock to make fire with. Get a boat at Tusket Falls and go for six miles. Ask for Jerry's Island. Good landing place on the north side.

There's one of 'em at Lake Rossignol on the Liverpool River, too, at the outlet of Rossignol. And at Musquodoboit Harbour, at the Jam Falls about one mile up the Musquodoboit River, there's a Grandmother rock. Sitting with her head toward the north. Yep. But no blanket. This Grandmother ain't wearing a blanket.

Another one is on Carleton Lake, what runs into Tusket River, the West Branch of the Tusket. It's on the east side of Carleton Lake. There are a lot of islands there, and Kukumijnawainoq is a rock there of granite. All them Grandmother rocks is granite. She faces north here. When the Indians visited this rock in their canoes, they always left something on the rock for Kukumijnawainoq. Indians always leave something — piece of meat or tobacco or punk. She was a great smoker, our Grandmother, and they always presented her with tobacco and punk. Then they would ask her for good luck for hunting. Punk is grown on a tree. Bulges out like a knot. It is very light. When the Indians would strike rocks to get a spark, they would have the spark fly onto the punk, and it would burn.

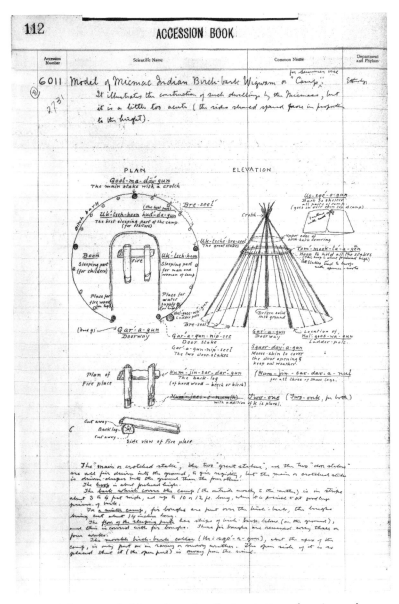

Harry Piers recorded Jerry Lonecloud's description of a wigwam's construction and the Mi'kmaw terms for its parts in Nova Scotia Museum Accession Book Three, 1927, page 112. (NSM, N-24,922 and N-24,92)

Locality and When Collected	Collector (c) Donor (d)	Received 1927	No. of Speci-mens.	Remarks
Made by Jeremiah Lone-cloud, Micmac Indian, Halifax, etc.; April 1927.	Bought from him for $8.00	22 Apr.	1	

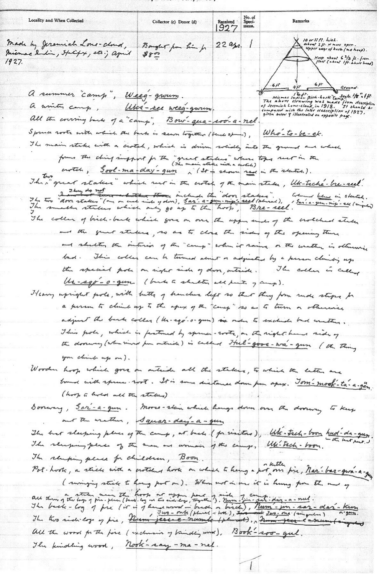

A summer "camp", <u>Weeg'-gwum</u>.

A winter camp, <u>Uks-see weeg-gwum</u>.

All the covering bark of a "camp", <u>Bow'-qua-soo'-a-nel</u>.

Spruce roots with which the bark is sewn together (hank of them), <u>Who'-to-be-ak</u>.

The main stake with a crotch, which is driven solidly into the ground and which forms the chief support for the "great stakes" whose tops rest in the crotch, <u>Sool-ma-day'-gum</u> (It is shown rest in the stakes).

The "great stakes" which rest in the crotch of the main stake, <u>Uk-tché'-bre-sel</u>. two
The two "door stakes" (one on each side of door), <u>Sar'-a-gum-nij'-sel</u> (stained),
The smaller stakes which only go up to the hoop, <u>Bre-sel</u>.

The collar of birch-bark which goes on over the upper ends of the crotched stake and the great stakes, so as to close the sides of the opening there and shelter the interior of the "camp" when it rains or the weather is otherwise bad. This collar can be turned about or adjusted by a person climbing up the special pole on right side of door, outside. The collar is called <u>Uk-agó'-o-gum</u> (bark to shelter all parts of camp).

Heavy upright pole, with butts of branches left so that they form rude steps for a person to climb up to the apex of the "camp" so as to turn or otherwise adjust the bark collar (Uk-agó'-o-gum) in order to exclude bad weather. This pole, which is fastened by spruce-roots, on the right-hand side of the doorway (when viewed from outside) is called <u>Hul'-goos-wa'-gum</u> (the thing you climb up on).

Wooden hoop which goes on outside all the stakes, to which the latter are bound with spruce-root. It is some distance down from apex. <u>Tom'-mook'-ta'-a-gen</u> (hoop to bind all the stakes)

Doorway, <u>Sar-a-gum</u>. Moose-skin which hangs down over the doorway to keep out the weather, <u>Squar-day-a-gum</u>.

The best sleeping place of the camp, at back (for visitors), <u>Uk-tch-boon hud-da-gum</u>.

The sleeping place of the men and women of the camp, <u>Uk-tch-boon</u>.

The sleeping place for children, Boon.

Pot-hook, a stick with a crotched hook on which to hang a kettle or pot over fire, <u>Nar'-bar-qua'-a-gen</u> (swinging stick to hang pot on). When not in use it is hung from the end of

a stick near the hoop at upper part of camp.
All three of the logs of fire, placed (back-log on two side-logs together), <u>Num-jin-sat-dar-a-nul</u>.
The back-log of fire (it is a large wood on back or brick), <u>Num-jin-sar-dar-kun</u>.
The two side-logs of fire, <u>Num-jese-e-numk</u> (plural), <u>Num-jese-e-num</u> (singular).
All the wood for the fire (inclusive of kindling wood), <u>Book'-soo-gul</u>.
The kindling wood, <u>Nook'-say-ma-nel</u>.

The Bird Ages

This story belongs to the Bird Ages. Two young Indian girls, sisters, strayed away. Got lost in the woods. Night overtook them, and they were obliged to stay all night under a spruce tree. It was a starlight night, and the oldest girl, peeking through boughs of the tree, saw two stars — one large, the other dim. She made a wish. She wished the stars were their husbands. She asked her sister to choose which she would have, the bright or dim. The younger sister said, "Which one did you wish?"

The older sister replied, "The small star which can just be seen."

So the younger sister said, "As long as you wish the small, I'll take the bright." Then they fell asleep.

In the morning, they found themselves in a strange land as the sun rose and glittered on rocks and trees and flowers. It was beautiful. They strolled along and had not gone far before they met an old lady who said, "Which of you wished the big star for a husband?" It was the youngest girl. The man appeared. He was old. The small star appeared. He was young.

The old lady said, "Here's your husbands. Husbands said they would be on duty all night as stars but will return in the morning and accompany you all day long." While the men were away, the old lady showed them around. They saw beauty such as they had not seen in the world from which they came. There was a flat stone with flowers around, and she warned them against going there. The oldest girl turned the stone over. She saw another place, the place where they came from. The lake with Indians going along in canoes. She called the youngest to look and see their home. She wished to return and tell them of this lovely place.

The old woman appeared and asked the oldest girl if she hadn't been told not to touch the stone. She said, "Yes, but I want to return to my people." Old lady said she would put veils over their faces and let them down. But no matter what they heard, they were not to remove the veils until they heard the Chipmunk.

As they went down, they heard the beautiful singing of the Wren. When they heard it, they thought they would like to see it. The oldest opened her veil, and they lit on a tall pine tree. When they lit on the tall pine tree, they wondered how they could get down. They saw a Bear passing by. They asked him if he would be so kind to take them down. He says, "No. I have no time. I have childrens at home, and I am in a hurry to go to them." So he went on.

It wasn't long before there was a Wolverine passing by. Wolverine is belonging to the Bear family, extinct in this country. First he refused. Says "No. How did you get up there? Can't you come down as well as you went up?"

They said, "We can't get down. Be so kind as to take us down, and you can have either one of us for your wife. Then the other one will be the second wife." He consented to take them down, and the oldest girl, she made this plan to unstring her hair-strings and tie them on those pine limbs, so they would be very difficult to untie if they wanted them. He took the girls down one by one, and the oldest girl says to him, "Oh, by the way, we forgot our hair-strings up there. Will you be so kind as to bring those down?"

The oldest girl made a wish for there to be wigwams there, filled with smoke and wasps' nests. So they ran away, and when he came down with the strings, the camp was already made, filled with those wasps' nests and smoke. He heard voices — "This way, this way, this way" — three times. When he opened the camp door, he heard the voices still, and he couldn't see them. But he threw himself in the direction where he heard the voices, and he busted the wasps' nests. Then he was chased out by the wasps, so he ran in the thicket to have those shaken off. After he got rid of the wasps, he found the girls were not in the camp. They had only put this in the wish to gain time to cross the river. Then he tracked them to the river, and he saw a Blue Heron standing by the river. He asked him, "Did you see two girls here?"

He said, "Yes. They're gone across on the other side."

The Wolverine asked him, "How did they get across?"

The Heron said, "I stretched my neck across the river, and they walked across on my neck to the other shore."

"Well then," the Wolverine said, "would you be so kind as to set me across, so I can overtake them?"

The Blue Heron said, "Yes." But on the way across, the Wolverine fell off the Heron's neck into the river. He couldn't swim. He had hopes to land on the shores of the side where they went, and instead of that, he landed on the same side where he started from.

People found him. They said, "Here's our old Uncle. He must have died long ago and been washed ashore. He's full of maggots." They saw him move, and he got up before them, shook the maggots off of him, and went up to the encampment. That ends him, the Wolverine.

As they were going to their home, the lost girls came to a lake, and they saw a canoe coming along the shore of the cove. They sang out to the person who was in the canoe. They wanted him to take them in the canoe. He asked them whereabouts they were going. The girls said, "We want to go to the outlet of the lake."

He says, "'Tain't my direction where I was going, but I'll take you down there." While they were in the canoe, there was some smoked dried meat he had in packages. The youngest girl, she was hungry, and she was nibbling those pieces of dried meat. The man of the canoe, he says, "Quit nibbling those dried meat."

Well, they got down to the foot of the lake to the encampment, a great encampment. And they all, as they landed, they all turned to birds. Those two girls were the prettiest sea birds. One was Wood Duck, as handsome a bird as we have in Nova Scotia. The other was Shell Duck, the second prettiest.

Well then, the Wood Duck, she gets married. One of those great birds took a great liking to her. The oldest one was the Wood Duck, and the younger was the Shell Duck. They were both going to get married with the best birds there in the outlet. Then they were asked where they belonged and who was their parents.

"Well," they said, "we belong here and our parents dwells here."

And when these pretty girls were asked about what was their family, they named their parents and were told that their parents died while their daughters were lost one hundred years ago. They fell to death. "Oh yes, a hundred years ago, they had two daughters who got lost and never was found."

This story belongs to the Bird Ages. The girls were human, and they turned into birds. This shows how the birds were formed from the human. This belongs to the Mi'kmaq legends going back thousands of years.

Jerry Lonecloud and his son Louis in 1921, posing with birch partridges at Climo Studios, Halifax. (NSM, N-5008)

The birds. Kluskap called all those people to him that he was going to transform.

Also those two girls who were in a trance for a hundred years or so. He said to the birds, "Now I'm going to give you headdresses. The two girls came from the sky, the happy hunting ground. He gave the oldest one the best headdress, and the second, the second best. There are Indian names for these girls: Wood Duck is named *Hawyawlkes.** Shell Bird, Whistler, is named *Kjikwej.* Wood Duck is prettiest bird we have in Nova Scotia or New Brunswick.

The birds were human, and Kluskap sent *Tities,* Blue Jay, to go up and inform the encampment that he was going to transform them into birds. He promised the Blue Jay the headdress if he would do this. Blue Jay went up and said, "Kluskap wants you to come down — all of you, and in canoes." All the duck families built the canoes and went down the lakes. They shot the rapids.

The last human to be transformed into a bird was *Plawej,* Partridge. She was the last to build a canoe, and she made it so perpendicular that when she launched it, it tipped over. It was narrowly built. She swam ashore. Her aim was to run all the way down the shores of the lake and shores of the river. When she came across the yellow birch twigs, she twisted those for suspenders to keep her stockings up. The withies of the yellow birch. She was the last to arrive where Kluskap was. All the head-dresses were gone, and she got none. She got a dress, and it was birch leaves, white and yellow birch, of two kinds sewed together. On the partridge's back, all these leaves are to be seen, well formed. Her tail feathers are in the form of the woods, spruce swamps, and birch hills.

When the Partridge got to where the headdresses were being distri-buted, the first birds there had got the prettiest headdresses — the Wood Duck and the Shell Duck. The rest come, and each one got their head-dresses except the Partridge, which was the last bird to arrive and had no headdress. The Partridge run around from one place to another, all through the wigwams of the bird encampment, to see if any bird happened to have two headdresses, so she could claim one. She was much disappointed, not getting one. She was willing to marry one of the birds if they wished.

Those with the prettiest headdresses said, "We will find a mate for you as far as we can do. The family bird will pick you out a man."

The Partridge was much disappointed when she found they had picked a Crow for her. She had a string of young ones — twelve or thirteen they have, generally. She had left them behind, but they followed her back and arrived at the bird encampment after she was married to the Crow because it took a good long time to find her.

They all humbled around her, and the old stepfather Crow did not like the idea of her bringing her little family. The old Crow got up a plan to snare those young partridges. He set snares for them, as they were running about all the time. He made the snares of little spruce roots. The snares had a tripper that would trip them up and hang them up in the air until they died. He did this one by one.

Partridge woman did not know what was going on until he had them all strung up. Then he told his wife. He put it on that the Partridge could not blame him. He said, "Oh, my! I was in the woods, and I saw every one of those young ones of yours hung up in the snare."

He got her to go down where the snares were and where they were hanging dead, and he was unconcerned who done it. At the same time, he done it, and he tried to get away with it. She did not know who to blame and did not blame the one who done it — her husband. But she was going to find out.

She said, "Now you stay home until I come back. I'm bound to find the one who did that, and I won't come back until I do find it." She told her husband, the Crow, "Now you got to forage, provide for yourself." She was a great provider but so crippled up with the thoughts of losing her young ones, she left him to do the best he could.

She never returned. She hunted away back until she came to her husband, the Partridge. They lived together again, and she told him all about how someone down there killed all her young'uns, and she was delayed coming back. She did not tell him of her marriage with the Crow.

So to this day, the Partridge has no headdress. Only the male bird had his cap on because he did not go for a headdress. The female threw her cap away as she came out of the water. She was in such a hurry to get this fine headdress of fine feathers, of beads, of shells, of bones.

The Owl was asked how she got those big eyes and could see so well in the night. "Oh," she said, "those are spectacles."

"What are they made of?"

"Isinglass," she said. "And I fasten them with wood frames. I can see with them better at night than in day."

Kluskap presented a wooden music made of sticks to each bird, so they can have their songs from those. The most beautiful one is the Brown Wren. It has only one note and is the best singing bird. The second best is the Swamp Robin — white way of calling it is the North American Thrush. It is the second best. It has three notes and is very remarkable. The other birds were given the same whistles to render their songs. But the songs of the different birds, loons, and ducks was all different. Kluskap made the promise to them, "When I come again, all those songs sung here should be sung in that great happy land I have prepared for you. There we shall be all together forever."

Kluskap says, "I am going to leave you here, and you shall all build your nests different from one another. There will be a good many enemies, and you will protect your young ones and teach them, and when I come for you, there will be no more enemies." This is the end of them bird stories.

When the animals and birds were human, Kluskap's niece was on the island, *Sighignish.** She was in the woods with a bow and arrows, shooting small game animals for prey. Squirrels, rabbits, and other small animals. When she returned, she found the people in the encampment had left in their canoes to go to the mainland when Kluskap required them to do that. She didn't know how to get onto the mainland. Finally she saw a Whale passing by. She said to the Whale, "Uncle, will you be so kind as to take me to the mainland? I am here all alone."

So he said, "Yes, I will take you, but I can't take you on dry land."

She said, "Well, take me as near as you can."

Every time the Whale would come up to take his breath, he says to her, "Do you see any sight of land yet?"

She disappointed him. She said, "No." All this time they were approaching the land, and first thing, he ran right up on the shore.

"Oh," she said. "Happened that you ran on dry land for me. But don't you mind, I'll get you off again." She took her bow and shoved him out into the sea again. And he was released. As she was travelling along the shore to find where Kluskap wanted the people to assemble, she saw something sticking out of the sand. She fired at the object with her bow and arrow. It was the knee of the Wolverine that fell off the bridge when he was chasing the two girls from the happy hunting grounds. She fired twice at the knee that was sticking up in the sand. She heard a voice when she fired but did not know where it was coming from. It was the Wolverine washed ashore.

When she came up to it, she said, "Oh Uncle, did I hit you?"

"Yes," he said, "but you didn't hurt me."

"Uncle, could you take me where Kluskap is?"

He said, "Oh yes. I'm going there."

"Well, that is where I want to go, too," replied Kluskap's niece, the Sable. "Will you be so kind as to take me there?"

The Wolverine said, "Yes."

When Wolverine brought her there, Kluskap had transformed these humans into animals: Moose, Caribou, Bear, Beaver, Lucifer, Wildcat, Fox, Fisher Cat, Mink, Weasel, Ground Mole, Deer, and Otter. Then he also transformed the Sable and the Wolverine into sable and wolverine.

Porcupine, Beaver and Water Mole

When animals were human, Porcupine was sulky and made no friends. Went his own way. He would not come with the rest to conferences. When Great Spirit put his curse on the animals, he allowed the Porcupine to go his own way. He don't bother anyone, and no one bothers him. He's of no use. That was the greatest curse that could be put on the Porcupine, to allow him to go his own way. Porcupine was working for that. He did not want to be any more than what he was. Everyone hated him. His curse was to keep that way. Porcupine has just one of a family. Never see old Porcupine with her young. She does not take care of it. Always, little Porcupine is alone.

Porcupine cuts popple, which is soft wood, maple, which is hard wood, and black alder and pussy willow boughs. Little Porcupine feeds on leaves and buds. In a month or so, he has same food as the old ones — goes to fir, juniper, or hemlock. Porcupine is hateful, hateful for herself and hateful for her young. Father Porcupine sleeps. A great fellow to sleep. You holler at him, and he looks up, sees what is going on, and shuts his eyes again. You never see two Porcupines together. They feed and go to a hiding place.

When it's wet, they'll go as long as a week without food. When it's fine, they'll come out. Don't do no work, nothing to do, and it is one of the animals without gall. Very queer. Porcupines don't like water. Don't go in water, don't go in rain. Curious ways. When there is a fire in the woods, the porcupine makes for the fire. It will go right in. In big woods fires, they will make for the fire. If they see a fire in the distance, they will go right in. Very curious this way.

Porcupine peels a tree with his teeth. Peels the rough part of the bark, and then feeds on the bark next to the wood, more suction than anything else. Then he goes up further and cuts the boughs. They fall to the ground, and he goes down and feeds on the green tips of boughs, spruce, hemlock, or fir.

After his meal on the ground, he makes for his resting place, which he has made in a log. He has three houses. He is liable to have a house of rock, or in the hollow of an old log, or under a log. He has no home, for he makes none. He makes no home but seeks one. He hunts for his hiding place. He does no work at all.

The Indian legend says the Porcupine is one of the laziest of the animals. Porcupines make no preparation for the winter. We don't look upon Porcupine as a smart person at all. He didn't work, didn't make no home, has no work to do, lives that way. A curse was put upon him to be slow, stupid, not intelligent.

Porcupine has one enemy called the fisher cat. Fisher cat is the only one outside the Indian who will attack a porcupine for food. This fisher cat eats porcupine. The fisher cat is grey-coloured and like an otter. But they are very rare now and are found chiefly in Labrador and Newfoundland. Their fur is very valuable, next in value to otter. No other animal outside the Indian will attack the porcupine. Porcupine has no friends.

Porcupines are hated by all other animals. Wildcats, wolves, bears, moose-deer, caribou-deer, and bear would all rather go round him than near him.

Now Beaver is intelligent. Legend says he built a canoe, and his tail formed the paddle. Beaver is more like an engineer, building a house and dam. When it is going to be a hard winter, Beaver has a double door, so if one freezes, he can get out another. In fall, Mother Beaver is left alone in the house. The others go away for the summer, down lakes, deadwaters, and brooks. They live on roots. In the fall, they gather wood for the winter food. They stick wood into the mud so they can easily get it in winter. Also gather pond-lily roots. Make the house of frame sticks. They use their tails for trowels to plaster the house with mud.

All them beavers winter together. They build dams to help them get their food way back in the swamps for winter, and they always provide for the winter. Nine beavers all have separate rooms in a beaver house. A full house is nine rooms, and everyone has his room and bed. They strip maple, alder, yellow birch, and wire birch for bedding. The beaver cuts the twig or stick and tows it on the water. No matter how big or how small, he tows it.

When he fells a tree, he always cuts it on the side near the water to his advantage. I saw a big black ash, fourteen inches across the middle. The beaver cut it off four or five feet from the ground, and it fell into the water and sank. The limbs he could cut under the water as well as he could on top, for the beaver can work underwater as well as he can on land. He cuts the limbs off and tows them to his winter quarters. Here he peels the bark and takes the sticks out of his house and away to be used in making the dam. He never uses a stick with bark on it for the dam.

Beaver — *Kopit* is his Indian name. The male Beaver is called *Gayay-dumsk**, and the female Beaver is called *Bulloomsk**. The Beaver's eldest son is called *Bullomscooitch**, and his youngest son, *Pilui'j*. The oldest daughter is *Goodgeebumcheeisch**." *Kopite'jk* means offspring of Beaver, male and female. There are generally nine in the whole family. *Kopitaq* means the outskirts of the family, or beavers in general.

Bags of castoreum, called *wisenawk** or *costimas,** are at the end of the beaver's tail. Indians use this as medicine. It has a scent, and when the beaver goes anywhere, the others can follow by scent. A nice scent or perfume it is.

Beavers can't protect themselves very well. They are easily caught, so every beaver house has a main guide — a water mole, small and dark like a muskrat, with a round tail like a common house rat. He is the main warner for enemies, and the beaver has a good many enemies: foxes, bears, wildcats, lynx — or lucifers, the French name for lynx. Water mole is not a beaver but a beaver's guide. He is a forerunner. He warns the beavers. One water mole lives with every beaver. He goes out and inspects the dam, way back where the water flows, and if there is any enemy approaching, he goes back to the beaver's home and notifies him not to come out. The beaver never comes out then.

If I go hunting and see that mole, or the mole sees or smells me, I know I'll get no beaver. Water Mole is beaver's guide. Indians fear him. Among our people, we fear him. If he sees us, no use to watch for the beavers that night. Beaver has no control of himself. He can't watch himself. When he cuts his wood, he does it whenever possible on a rainy night when the bears and foxes don't come out because they don't like to get wet. Beaver has a road to haul his wood to the water. But he only uses this path on a dull or rainy night. Other times he works at the edge of the water. But on a long haul, he uses only the wet nights. He has that much knowledge. He does not trust himself. He trusts the Water Mole.

I heard old people years and years ago talking about Water Mole, but one was never known to be killed. He can't be killed because he's a witch. The little mole, he tells him all. *Kopituk-puoinal,* beaver-witch. It is a mystery where he comes from. Beaver has a flat tail, and a Water Mole has a round tail like a common rat, not like a muskrat. Water Mole's fur is very fine and very black, different from the fur of a beaver.

I know of no history about the water mole, but the beaver always has him for his guide. Every beaver house has a water mole, but where they came from I don't know. *Alamaske'j* is the Mi'kmaq for mole. Mole is bound to see what is going on. When I cut a beaver's house open, all the beavers have fled. The separate rooms were all around the house, but the water mole was in the centre room. That centre room is now named after the Water Mole. Called the *samuqwaney alamaske'j,* which means Water Mole.

Insects and Frogs

When insects were great, the Ant was the noblest and strongest and acted as chief of the insects. If any animals or fish were brought into the encampment, it was his duty to divide it among the insects. Whatever the insects killed, they brought it to him, and he distributed it among them.

The insects killed a whale with bow and arrows. They drug him ashore away on the mainland with twisted withies. The Ant thought he would work a plan whereby he would only give the whale away to his own family. When a good many of the insects came for their share of the whale, the Ant seized them and twisted their necks so he could have it all.

When he had killed so many, the insects got alarmed. One Kinap insect, who had bigger power than all the insects put together, got news of it. He says, "I'll go down and net him." And he went down and seized the Ant. He said, "I understand you're killing people." Insects were people at that time. "You've done wrong, and I'm going to divide this up." So he cut the whale up and gave it away to the poorest class of insects. Kinap, the greatest of the insects, cut the whale's head off. He divided everything but that. It was all that was left. He says to the chief Ant, "That is your share. The head."

The Ant replied, "That's just what I wanted."

This Kinap Insect says, "You eat that, and you can live in it. When you've got it all et, you can have it for your house, because you're a great carver." Ant is a great carver of wood. He can cut wood in any shape. After he had eaten all the meat off it, he used it for a house and had many rooms in it. Kinap said to the Ant, "In the winter, you'll freeze to death, but you'll come to in the spring."

So it is to this day. The ant freezes in the tree. Water runs in a knothole in a tree, and he is covered in ice and frozen stiff but comes to in the spring. I often cut wood for the fire and found ants frozen in the wood. When they get near the fire, they come to. The ant enjoys the summer but is dead in the winter. This was his punishment for being greedy.

Emperor Moth is the biggest butterfly we have. He was one of the biggest insects we know of. He just sings around and does not store any provisions to eat. In the wintertime, he goes around to the other insects, to the ants. The Ant forages all summer and provides food for the winter. This Locust — first it's a locust, and then it's a butterfly — goes and begs from the Ant when the winter come. And the little Ant refused the Locust.

The Ant said, "What were you doing all summer?"

The Locust said, "I was singing all summer."

Said the Ant, "I can't help you. If you think you could get along, you could sing away."

And he could get nothing to eat then, so the Locust went to the Chipmunk, a striped animal. The Chipmunk gathered food for the winter. He told the Locust, "I heard you singing last summer. I thought you had plenty in store for your winter, so I can't give you any, as I have only enough for my offspring."

So the Locust kept on singing all through the summer. He said, "I am going to turn myself into a worm and spin a cocoon and go without eating all winter. In the spring, I will turn into a flying insect, a butterfly." Later on he laid an egg, which hatched into a locust, which sings all summer. The Locust arranged it so that he would not have to work in the summer or eat in the winter, but so that he could sing all summer.

Sinmaju loved all them insects, reptiles, animals, and birds. He was their god. And they loved him because he saved them from the flood. He took reptiles — four or five different kinds of snakes, newts, lizards — into the iceberg. He took the tree peep frog, the smartest frog, who goes up in the tree about September and stays until it is cold enough for him to hunt his winter quarters. He took frogs, toads, and pollywogs.

When Sinmaju placed the animals, reptiles, birds, frogs, and toads in the iceberg, he provided them their foods. He made a storeroom for the reptiles, frogs, toads, and flies, all in one room, so they could be provided with food along with the big animals. Also he provided foods for his family, his sons and himself. He provided meats and fish for this great flood. He didn't know how long it would be that way, but he foresaw the flood, and no one of the other tribes believed there would be such a thing.

All the intelligent race of people found weren't in Noah's Ark. The Indians wasn't.

Long before the flood, it is understood that the Snake was a human. He told a lie, and he was punished, and he crawled.

Before the flood, before he become a frog, the Frog was the head man of the water.

He had charge of the lakes that supplied the encampment with water. He was very stingy with the water. He would make complaints about what they were doing with the water. He thought they were wasting it, coming so often, and he refused to serve a good many with water. So they informed Kluskap about it.

Kluskap sent an animal called *Wowkwis*, the fox, to try him and see if he would refuse him water. Wowkwis was one of Kluskap's water carriers. He returned to Kluskap without any. This man Frog said it was dry time, and he couldn't share any more water. Kluskap then sent the Blue Heron to pierce the dam where the water was kept. The dam burst, and a great flood of water that Frog had been keeping back came forth. So all had a big supply of water. Kluskap told the Blue Heron to hit Frog on the back. Kluskap then transformed him into a frog, and this is the reason he has a hump on his back from that blow from the Heron.

Before the flood, the Pollywog was sitting by a lake, and a Raven came along. This was before the Raven was transformed from a human into a raven. Raven asked Pollywog what he was doing there. Pollywog answered:

I am going down
Into the water
Where there are no stars.

Which he did. He then turned into a Pollywog — not the pollywog that turns to a frog, but the real Pollywog that never comes to the surface.

Biting flies such as blackflies, mosquitos, midges, and great big moose flies — these come from a bone of the cannibals that existed before the flood. The flood killed them. The nature of the cannibals was that they used to eat people. When Sinmaju formed the iceberg, he put the flies on.

We were not in Noah's ark. We had our own ark.

Sinmaju prophesied the flood. When the Indians killed Kukwes, the great giant cannibal, they burnt him up and powdered up his bones. To destroy him, the Indians blew the dust of Kukwes's bones into the air. Although he was dead and burnt, Kukwes said in his mind, "This dust of my bones, let it turn to flies and eat people." Which was done, so we still have the pest of Kukwes in the woods. We say, "Well, it was Kukwes's wish."

Moose and Caribou

Moose always has a browsing place. It is called his yard. He feeds to windward. He turns to the left and lies down to leeward where he started from so he can smell his enemy. Knows a day beforehand which way the wind will be, Indian says. Moose eats fir, spruce, hemlock, withrods, short moosewood, short yellow birch, maple, and frogwood. Frogwood has red poison berries. Indians deceive moose by standing over smoke from a fir or spruce fire for a few minutes. Moose does not run from this.

In summer, he selects muddy swampy places where he can roll around in mud and protect himself from flies. He is that cute. He feeds in summer on blue water lilies — moose lilies — in lakes or deadwaters. He wades out and gets them. He also nips yellow lilies and white lily flowers. Moose selects an island or some point in a lake, the point where the water runs out.

When he hears an enemy coming, he lifts his leg and shakes his hoof. It rattles, like click, click, and this noise is a signal. Travels like a telephone. It rings in the other moose's ear like a telephone and gives the signal to go away. But before the moose runs, he looks in the direction of his fellow moose. This gives the hunter his cue. He need only follow the moose's look.

When Kluskap transformed Moose from a person to a moose, he said, "You aren't going to eat any meat or fish or fruit or berries." Moose were sent out by twos, in pairs, man and woman.

They said, "We don't know what to do. Kluskap commanded us not to eat meat or fish or berries of any kind."

Moose twisted a yellow birch twig. He tasted it, and it tasted nice. He gave it to his wife and said, "Taste this, and I will get some more." These twigs had good substance. They fed on the yellow birch until it got scarce and out of their reach. They then tried maple twigs. They said this had

Jerry Lonecloud and 97-year-old Chief Peter Wilmot at the Hector Celebration, Pictou, 1923. Lonecloud is carrying the skull and antlers of a moose which Wilmot shot when he was in his eighties; he lived to be over a hundred. (NSM, N-5675)

good substance, too. They thought most every bush would be good for them. He tried withrod and spruce tops. They found great substance in spruce tops and the tops of young firs. So all the twigs they could reach was their food in wintertime. In summer, when the leaves came out, they fed on tips of all the leaves of the trees they could reach. Then they began on the low stuff — on a herb, now named for them, moose-tongue.

When they feed their young, they give them moose-tongue. It is so soft and nice, with moisture. So they eat herbs of different kinds in the low plants. They also eat water plants in the lakes and coves, and tips of lily plants. There is a blue lily called the moose lily. They wade out and eat it in July, before it gets tough. They also eat white lily tips and yellow lily tips. So the Moose lives well, as well as any of us, even if he doesn't eat meat, fish, fruit, or berries.

The killing of the Moose by the Birds, it was a great undertaking. Chickadee, a small bird about as big as your thumb, proposed it. He said, "Let's go and kill that Moose." But it looked very impossible. Meatjay, or Butcherbird, Robin, Crow, Blue Jay, and Chickadee, they started out. Chickadee selected the Moose they were going to kill. So they went all together on this great long weary chase through the woods and into the lake and out of the lake. The Moose took to water and thought he would get clear of them, but they flew over him until he landed on the opposite shore.

The chase commenced again, and everyone had a pick at him. They worried the Moose, and he couldn't eat. In the night when the birds retired was the only time he could eat. In the morning at daylight, they were at it again. The Moose was very fresh in the morning because he had eaten at night, and he put up a great fight to get away.

The Crow said, "I'll pick his eyes out." So he did. The Moose was worried because he couldn't feed that night, but the Birds retired just the same. In the morning, they found him just where they left him the night before. Then they all turned to, picked him to death, and fed off him. Robin, he fell out. He did not chase. He liked the fire they had made, and he stayed by it. The other four et the Moose.

The Chickadee went out and said to the Eagle and Raven that he had killed a Moose and was going to have a great feast and invite all the birds to come. So they all came, and the Eagle and the Raven, Crow and Meatjay

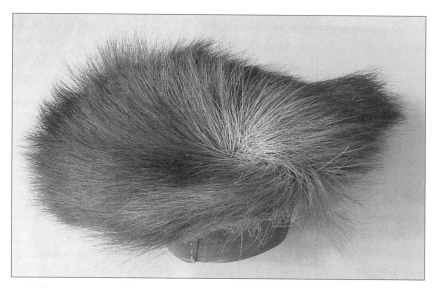

Mi'kmaw cap made by Jerry Lonecloud in 1916, from the bell and part of the neck-skin of a bull moose he had killed, attached to a birchbark headband. Peter Charles, an elder who died before 1880, had told him these were worn by Mi'kmaw men long ago. (NSM)

began to carry away the Moose and hide it in different places so they could have it when they wanted it. They left only the skeleton of the Moose for the Chickadee. "Oh, that'll be enough for him," they said. To this day, the Chickadee picks the bones. He gets a certain substance out of it. The Chickadee would go to their hiding places. He was very particular about his food. He ate only the fat. He left the lean meat for the others. After the food was gone, the birds wondered when the Chickadee would kill another Moose. They gave him the credit for it.

The Chickadee said, "Let the next lucky one try his luck, and I'll take the offal."

The Eagle killed the small game — young moose, young rabbits, young partridges, young beavers, young muskrats. The Chickadee would have his share. The Eagle would kill because he was the biggest bird. The others would eat the offal, and they do this to the present day. Even if Indians kill, they go for what is left on a moose, caribou or bear. The Eagle was the second lucky one.

We never could leave a moose-kill for two or three days, as the birds would have it all carried away.

Caribou. Their feeding ground is bogs or savannahs. They feed on different kinds of moss in the bogs, mostly the moss that is named after them, caribou moss. It's white, and grows in clusters. When they have their young, they take them out on the bogs and feed them on caribou moss. They generally go there after a rainstorm, and the rain moistens the caribou moss so the young can eat it. They also eat moss off trees such as white maple, rock maple, spruce, and fir. They always go up against the wind so they can scent their enemies: lucifer, bigger than wildcat; wildcat; bear; wolverine, and the Mi'kmaq, their biggest enemy of all.

Caribou never believes his own eyes. If he sees his enemy, he must be sure, so he'll go up to it. Must come around three times when he sees you. The Mi'kmaw man hunting the caribou chops some brush and carries it before him. Sometimes the bog is a mile long and a mile wide. The Caribou sees the bush move and investigates. When within gunshot, the Mi'kmaq plant the bush in front of them and shoot. I have seen a herd of thirty, and the leader come the closest. If you're hidden from him, the others come. They are simple that way. If you keep behind your little brush, you can shoot so many as you want. They'll hang around. They are simple this way, and that's why they are now so scarce.

Ki'kwa'ju, the Tricky Wolverine

The Wolverine, Ki'kwa'ju, is very tricky to the other birds and animals. He gets all kinds of games on them. Before the winter sets in, all the Indians and animals that don't go around in the wintertime so much gather their food and store it away. The Wolverine knew all this and depended upon this to get food off the others. He was lazy himself and wouldn't gather food for himself. He went to the Bear in the winter, but the Bear had nothing to eat — he sleeps all winter. Wolverine could get nothing there. The Bear told him it was best to hunt himself a den and winter there, sleep it out. He did so. But he got tired of this before spring and thought he would do like the Indians and kill moose, smoke it, and dry it for the winter. Also beaver meat. He would smoke and dry it for the winter. And birds — fowl.

Next fall he started in. But he could not get up courage to kill the animals because they were too big. So he started in on birds. He built a great wigwam and told the birds, "We are going to have a great meeting here. I want all you birds to come to this great meeting I'm going to have."

The different birds came at this appointment. After he got them into the wigwam, he sat them all around the camp. In the middle was an open space. There's where he addressed the birds: "Now I'm going to tell you one of the greatest things that's going to happen. I want all youse to listen and close your eyes and not to open your eyes, because if you do you lose your eyesight. No matter what you hear, do not open your eyes." This was his way to get his supply of birds for the winter.

He came to the first bird and took hold of it by the head and threw it in the middle space. They all heard the flapping. He did the same to the next bird and threw this in the middle. He threw everyone he took hold of in the centre likewise, and there was quite a noise of screeching and flapping of wings. A good many thought they would like to see what this noise was about and what was going on, but no one dared look because they were told they would lose their eyesight. At last the Loon thought, "I'll just open one of my eyes to see. I don't care if I lose that one." He opened his eye, saw those birds with their heads twisted off. He sang out, "Open your eyes, all get out, he's going to kill us all." So all flew away, and Wolverine got very few.

Since that time, when you see a loon, you generally see he has one eye closed. This is the eye he thought he was going to lose. But he can see with both eyes. This didn't work for the Wolverine.

Then the Wolverine went to his den. He began to rob the birds' nests and catch the young birds and young animals. Next he stole the provisions the Indians would lay away. They stored their food in a wooden hut. The Wolverine would dig underneath and steal the food. This worked all right. They did not miss the food until the Wolverine was already in his den and the Indians couldn't get him. He never tried the same hut twice. Because the Indians laid traps.

When the Indians made an eel weir to catch eels, usually in the night, they split them and smoked them on a scaffold to dry for the winter. The Wolverine would come and lug great back-loads through the night. Towards daylight, he wouldn't go there again, for he knew the Indians would be on the watch with bows and arrows and tomahawks. He would return in another way, but not take the eels off the scaffold, for he would know there were traps made there for him. He would go to the eel pot, take it out of the water, dump it in a place, and then take a back-load of those. When he would be going past the scaffold where he stole before, there would be hanging up a large body of eels. Very tempting, but he wouldn't go there.

He would go where the Indians had been killing a moose, bear or caribou, and take the best of what they left. When the Indians came back for their meat, it would be gone, and they would know who had taken it.

The great Eagle, Kulu, heard of Ki'kwa'ju doing these evil things, stealing from the people, and Kulu went to see him. But the Wolverine always got out of his way as much as he could. At last Kulu met him when he was coming from a long point onto the mainland. Kulu said, "You're the one I want to see. You're just the one I'm after, and I want to see how you've been playing so many tricks on those poor people. I'm going to carry you away. I'm going to carry you up to the star where you came from."

Ki'kwa'ju knew he couldn't get away, so he said, "Oh yes, I wanted to go there long ago. I'm tired of this ground. The star named Chickadee told me about where we came from long ago, and I'm glad I'm going."

While Kulu was ascending, Ki'kwa'ju said, "Is this all the far it is? Keep going with me. I wanted to go there long ago."

Kulu thought he couldn't do him any injury, couldn't punish him by taking him up to the star. So he thought when they got out of sight of the world, he would let him go, and he would be dead before he reached the earth. Ki'kwa'ju said to Kulu, "Is the world still in sight?"

Kulu answered, "I will let you know." So when the world was out of sight, he said, "Now it's out of sight, and I'm going to let you go."

While he was going down, Ki'kwa'ju gave a wish to himself: "I wish my backbone would be left when I strike the ground. Then the ants will gather me up." He knew he would be crumpled up. He knew he'd likely strike the

Rocky Mountains. "So I'll be whole again. So I can rove around the old hunting ground once more." He got his wish. This was in the winter.

Ki'kwa'ju came across the Marten. The Marten was a great tobogganer, very fond of coasting. He had a great toboggan. Ki'kwa'ju, back to his trick only in a different way, said, "Oh, by the way, lend me your toboggan." Old Mrs. Porcupine was there. Ki'kwa'ju said, "I want to give this old lady a coast down to her home." She lived among the rocks in the caves, so he got her on the toboggan.

The Marten said, "Oh, by the way, I'll coast down with you, so I'll have my toboggan." It was a very long hill and many trees in the way, but Ki'kwa'ju was a very good coaster, much better than the Marten. While he was steering down the hill, the Marten got very uneasy. Thought Ki'kwa'ju would strike a tree while he steered it away from one tree to another. The Marten became so uneasy that when they were going by a big tree, he mounted the tree. He thought they would strike a tree and be all killed.

Old Mrs. Porcupine was also afraid they would be killed. She said, "You need not go all the way. Steer to one side, and I'll walk the rest of the way." But instead of steering away from the cave, Ki'kwa'ju made a bee line for it. At the entrance to the cave, Mrs. Porcupine fell out and slid right into the cave. Just before they struck the rocks, Ki'kwa'ju jumped clear, and the toboggan smashed to pieces.

The Marten came down, crying about his toboggan. Ki'kwa'ju said, "Don't you cry. I'll make you one and bring it over to you." So he stopped at that.

When he came home to his parents in the encampment, the Marten said, "I saw Ki'kwa'ju."

"Oh," the old people said, "it couldn't be him because Kulu took him up to the stars, and he has not been heard of since." So the boy, Marten, was doubted, and Ki'kwa'ju did not replace the toboggan but got away.

This was towards spring. The Indian trappers set up their traps. Deadfalls. Beaver deadfalls, wildcat deadfalls, bear deadfalls. Ki'kwa'ju used to go to see their traps, take out the animals from the deadfalls, and place an old stick of wood in them for a trick. He would take away the animals. Most every trap he came to, he would do this. His old tricks, only a different way. When the trappers came home, they reported missing animals and sticks of wood instead in the deadfall. They said, "This is like the time Ki'kwa'ju was here before the Eagle took him away. This might be another one but can't be, as there was only one, and he was taken away."

Finally they found his tracks in a muddy swamp. They decided to set snares on every road. When Ki'kwa'ju came to a path, he would not go across it or follow it up or down but followed it up by the side of a path to the end, then swung to the other side and followed it down. Then moved to another section, where he would do the same trick, take an animal from the trap. So it was learned he was back, but how he got back was a mystery.

Later on, he took animals from the steel traps. He always took all the meat he could and destroyed the rest. He made it awful for everyone to use by rolling it in the mud. The Indians said, "When the snow comes, we'll be sure to find his track and kill him then."

But Ki'kwa'ju always knew when there was a storm coming. He was a regular barometer. And then he would make for his den. At the first light snow, just before he went to his den, if he saw there was a storm coming, he would go to a thicket and walk backwards to his den.

When the Indians arrived, they would say, "He's gone out. There's his track going out." And did not bother to look in. They would follow the track to a thicket. By then a storm would be up, and snow would cover the tracks. Bear does the same thing. Tracks himself backwards, jumps to one side, and goes back again to his den. All the wolverines finally disappeared and are now found in Labrador. Still tricky, it is said.

Just of late years, up to Miramichi, the old people were telling me of a wolverine that would come out when they were tapping the maple trees for sap. The wolverine would turn the birchbark or wooden troughs upside down, so there would be no sap in them when the Indians returned. He would then go all through the camp. Next week the Indian got a hardwood fire and buried the coal with ashes. He left a powder horn full of powder in the camp when they went out. The wolverine went through the troughs and birchbark dishes. When he went into the camp, he struck the end of the powder horn in the coals and blew himself up. He got blind and was alive when the Indians returned. This is the last wolverine to be got — over fifty years ago. The skin was sold in Saint John.

Ki'kwa'ju always heard a lobster would bite very hard, which it does. So one day when the tide was going out and it was nearly low tide, he went down and found a lobster in a hole in a mud bank. His claws were out — forward. Ki'kwa'ju was very careful with water. He did not like to get wet, so he said to himself, "I'll get a long stick and prod the lobster while he is in his hole." He prodded and prodded until he thought he had him in pieces. "Now I'll see how hard you can bite." So he put his toe into the hole. The lobster grabbed it and bit him

This story of the Wolverine blowing himself up was told to John Gyles, an English boy, during his captivity with the Maliseet in New Brunswick, beginning about 1687.

very hard. Ki'kwa'ju begged for him to let him go, but this lobster paid no heed to that, and the tide was coming up. Still he begged for him to let him go until the tide came over his shoulders. Ki'kwa'ju almost drowned. At last he said he would never hurt any of the lobster family any more, so he was let free.

There once was a bird named *Wikwa'sun'kwejit.* Means a bird flapping his wings and making wind or frost. Wikwa'sun'kwejit means a windmill, making high winds. This bird lives on the top of the mountain, and when he flaps his wings, they make high winds, gales, hurricanes, and whirlwinds. Ki'kwa'ju went up to him and said, "Oh, Grandfather, will you come down handier to the seashore?" Ki'kwa'ju imagined he could fly down.

But Wikwa'sun'kwejit replied, "No, I can't without help."

Ki'kwa'ju said, "Oh, I'll help you." The Old Man was willing to be helped down. So Ki'kwaju took Wikwa'sun'kwejit by the wing, and when they got just about halfway down the mountain, Ki'kwa'ju slipped and fell among the rocks, and Wikwa'sun'kwejit broke his wing. Ki'kwa'ju did this on purpose, but he pretended to be very sorry, and they managed to get to the seashore. He was going to play a trick on the Heron, Fish Hawk, and Eagle.

When Wiwa'sun'kwejit got down, Ki'kwa'ju said, "I want you to flap your wings to ruffle the water so they can't see the fish in the bottom."

Wikwa'sun'kwejit said, "I can't do that. My wing is broken, so I can't ruffle the water as you want."

Ki'kwa'ju said, "I'll put on a splint and tie it up." He did this, which enabled Wikwa'sun'kwejit to ruffle the water so the Heron, Fish Hawk and Eagle couldn't see the fish.

Then Ki'kwa'ju saw he was injuring himself because when the Fish Hawk would get fish, he would take it to his nest for the young, and Ki'kwa'ju would go up and steal it. He did not notice this until the Hawk got no fish. Then Ki'kwa'ju said to Wikwa'sun'kwejit, "Don't you flap your wings any more." So the water became calm, and the Fish Hawk, Heron, and Eagle saw the fish plainly.

While the wind was off, the bottom of the shores had become stagnated and covered with seaweed and eel grass, so the fish couldn't be seen. Ki'kwa'ju wasn't satisfied with this, so he said to Wikwa'sun'kwejit, "Flap your wings again to make rough water to drive this dirty stuff away." The Old Man did so, and the fish could be seen plainly on the bottom.

This was ended by Kluskap, who said to the Wolverine and the Old Man, "Now you go about your own ways and hunt for yourselves."

Ki'kwa'ju, Wolverine, is quite a prominent person in the Indian legends. He appears a great many times.

Apli'kmuj, the Visiting Rabbit

Indian name of Rabbit is *Apli'kmuj*. Apli'kmuj was a great visitor, and every place he visited, they would give him a feast. He never took his wife with him. First he visited the Bear. Bear gave him a great feast with plenty of fat meat. After he got his great feast, he said to the Bear, "You come and visit me." So after a time, the Bear went and visited the Rabbit. The Rabbit said to his wife, "You put on the pot to cook." She said she had nothing to cook.

"I have got nothing to eat?"

"No."

"Well now," he said, "I'll have to cut a piece off you." He put that in the pot, but there was no fat at all. It was dry. The Bear had treated him to fat meat, all the best. The Rabbit told the Bear to come again, and he would be prepared for him.

The Rabbit went to visit the Otter. The Otter, he cut a hole in the ice and speared the eels. The eels and trout and perch were cooked for the Rabbit visitor, and he had a good feast. After the feast was over, the Rabbit said, "Now you come and visit me. I want you to come over."

The Otter said, "I'll come some day."

So the Otter came one day to visit the Rabbit. The Rabbit said to his wife, "Now the Otter is here, I want you to cook some fish."

She said, "We have no fish."

He said, "Well then, I'll go and get some fish." He was going to try and do like the Otter did — fish with a spear. But he had no spear, and he dove down in the hole in the ice. He couldn't stay down. He floated up and didn't get no eels. Then they had nothing to eat for the Otter. The Rabbit went several times into the hole, and the old woman said, "You'll drown yourself if you don't come in." So the Otter went home without anything to eat.

Rabbit went to visit the Woodpecker, the English Black Woodpecker, biggest pecker of all. Indian name *An'tawe'j*. An'tawe'j flew up on the tree, picked there, picked eats out of the wood, and gave the Rabbit a great feast also. After the feast was over, the Rabbit said to An'tawe'j, "You come and visit me."

So An'tawe'j visited the Rabbit one day. The Rabbit made a wooden bill for himself, and he was going to do as An'tawe'j did. Jump on the tree and see if he could pick eats out of the tree. When An'tawe'j came, the Rabbit said to his wife, "Oh, you put the pot on. We give An'tawe'j a feast."

She said, "We have nothing to cook."

"Oh," he said, "I'll get some." He had the wooden bill already made. He fastened it on his nose, and then he mounted the tree and picked. But he got nothing, only sore mouth.

The old woman said, "Oh, you come down off the tree. You must have seen somebody doing that and are trying to imitate him." So An'tawe'j went back without getting any feast.

The Rabbit said, "Well now, I'm going hunting, and I'll have something ready to eat, ready for when we have company." First thing he came across young Lynxes. The Father and Mother Lynx were away, so the Rabbit took advantage and killed the young Lynxes and et them all. After he had his feast, he did not know what to do. He did not want to go home. He knew the Father Lynx would be after him. So he went in a different direction from his home in order to get away from the Lynx.

He came across a large spruce swamp. He marked the swamp up in tracks. He went in every direction, every which way. He knew the Lynx would be after him, and it would be difficult to trace him to where he was. He tired himself out and was obliged to sit under a tree. The Lynx tracked him to the tree. He said, "You're Rabbit. Just the man I want. You killed my young ones and et them."

"Oh no, I ain't the Rabbit. I saw a Rabbit pass by here just before you came."

The Lynx said, "Well, I'll go and retrack him again."

While the Lynx was gone, the Rabbit had a chance to escape. The Lynx tracked him up again to the spot where he saw him under the tree. "Oh," he said, "that was the Rabbit. That was him. Now he's gone. He fooled me. Now he ain't going to fool me again."

The Rabbit had one day gained on him, on the Lynx, and he came to another big spruce swamp; he tracked that all up also. Then he sat under a tree again. When the Lynx came up to him, the Rabbit made the tree a wigwam. He was holding a council in it. He disguised himself by putting a white blanket over his shoulders. The Lynx came up. He tracked him to the door and was sure the Rabbit was in there now. So the Lynx went up to the councillor, the Rabbit. He said, "You are the Rabbit at last."

But Rabbit denied it again. "Well," he said, "I'm the chief of this tribe here."

The Lynx said, "He must be in here because I've tracked him to the door."

The Rabbit said, "He was here, but he has gone away." The Lynx had to re-track him again. Had the same trouble over again. This gave the Rabbit another day in the race ahead of the Lynx.

When the Lynx came up to the spot where he saw the Rabbit with the gown on, he said to himself, "I'm sure that was the Rabbit I was speaking to. Now I'm going to track him, and wherever I find him, I'm going to kill him and eat him."

So the Rabbit made a beeline for the lake. He knew then he was going to be caught, and he didn't know what to do. He made for the lake. When he got to the shore of the lake, he threw a dry stick into the water and jumped on it. He floated out into the lake. He knew the Lynx wouldn't swim, but he was on the dry stick and used to walk back and forward on it. He disguised himself as an officer and the stick as a man-of-war.

He got quite a piece off in the lake, and when the Lynx saw him, he said, "Oh, it's a good thing you are so far off in the lake. You know I can't swim after you."

The Rabbit said to his warriors, "You get that big bow and arrow out, and I'll fire the arrow at that Lynx if he doesn't get away from the shore." So the Lynx had to run away.

He turned back and said to the Rabbit, "Wherever you wash ashore, you'll eat wood for the remainder of your days."

So the Rabbit lives on bark and twigs to this day.

The Great Powers

Earthquake, an Indian man, and his wife lived thousands of years ago. They died and left a family of a daughter and a son, Young Earthquake and Miss Earthquake. They thought they were the only two in the world and they were the wonder of the world. Young Earthquake went hunting. Game was very scarce, and he would be gone all day and perhaps get only enough to last overnight. Miss Earthquake kept the wigwam and got very lonely over time. She said to her brother, "Can't you hunt a companion for me while you are away, so I could have someone to talk to?"

He replied, "I don't know of anyone I could get. Father and Mother did not tell me there was anyone else. Did they tell you?"

She said, "No. I'm asking you."

He says, "I'll go and see if I can get you a companion. I'll go to the rising sun, east." Then he went to work and got Miss Earthquake provisions enough to last two years. He says, " I'll go one year to the rising sun, and it will take another year to come back."

After he got the provisions required for two years, he took his bow and arrow in the morning and fired the arrow east. He would go where the arrow fell. This he continued all day. His intention was that there was someone there with the sun to make the sun come up and go down. When the sun went down, he was then obliged to stop all night. Next day he continued to fire the arrow eastward, and when he would come up to it, he would fire it further on.

The second night, he heard a curious noise ahead, a sound he had never heard before. Next morning he thought he would reach that place before long. Still he was firing the arrow and getting up to it. The third evening, he heard a little plainer the sound. It was a tom-tom, the Indian music. At sundown, he came upon a wigwam, and here was where the tom-tom sounded. When he got up to the front of the wigwam, he saw a man dancing round and round inside. As he approached to the door, the man saw him and invited him in. This man was the evil spirit Mi'kmwesu.[2]

Mi'kmwesu invited Young Earthquake to the best part of the wigwam, and after they sat down, Mi'kmwesu asked Young Earthquake where he was going. Young Earthquake replied, "I am hunting a companion for my sister, and I don't know where to go. Perhaps you could tell me."

The Mi'kmwesu says, "I don't know of anyone, only *Kaqtukwaq*, Thunders. They have a daughter. Perhaps you could get her for your companion and also for your sister."

Earthquake replied, "Could you go with me to the place where the Thunder is?"

The Mi'kmwesu answered, "Yes. I will do my best for you." So they started on their journey. They hadn't gone very far before they came on a big hardwood hill. Then they saw a man standing on top of the hill. The Mi'kmwesu ran up to the strange man and said, "Why are you standing here?" The man had his nostrils plugged with two sticks. Mi'kmwesu said, "What is that for?"

The man answered, "If I let one of those loose, a big whirlwind would come and twist the trees from the roots and take them up to the sky."

The Mi'kmwesu said, "I should like to see that. Just loose one of those sticks out of your nostrils and I'll see." And it was done.

The whirlwind came and twisted the trees and also took this Mi'kmwesu up. He heard a voice in the sky saying twice, "Plug your nostrils. Plug your nostrils." And the Mi'kmwesu fell to the ground.

Mi'kmwesu said to the man with his nostrils plugged, "You are just the man we want to go with us to the Thunder family. Young Earthquake is going to marry Miss Thunder."

The man with great power in his nostrils was willing to go. This made them three.

They hadn't gone very far before they came upon another hardwood hill and saw a man standing on top of the hill. The Mi'kmwesu ran up and asked him, "What are you doing here?"

This man replied, "I am the Heat Lightning. I could go around the world before you could smoke the pipe of tobacco out." The Heat Lightning man had his knee tied up. He said, "I have to tie my leg to keep from running away. If I have both legs free, I would not be able to keep myself from running as fast as I can away off round the world in no time."

Mi'kmwesu said he would like to see that done. He said, "I'll load the pipe, and then I will light it."

Heat Lightning replied, "I will loosen my knee when you light the pipe." When the pipe was lit, Heat Lightning disappeared out of sight and returned before Mi'kmwesu had the pipe smoked. Then he tied up his knee again.

Mi'kmwesu said, "We would like to have you come with us to the great wedding on Thunder Island." Heat Lightning consented to go.

All started together and had not gone far before they heard a man chopping. They came up to this good man. He had cut down seven long pines, trimmed.

Mi'kmwesu ran after this man and said, "What are you going to do with those pines, whole length trees?"

"I am getting wood for an encampment over here." The man shouldered those pines and threw them to the front of a great wigwam and showed him. "I am getting wood for this man in the wigwam." He invited those great men into the wigwam and all entered. It was a great spirit's wigwam — Kluskap.

All this time Kluskap knew all about this because he was a great spirit, and he invited them all to sit down in the wigwam. He had a servant, a great servant, to cook for these men. He put on great pots, three of them.

While the water was boiling, he put his hand behind him. He was sitting on some brush. He hauled out a little bone, which he scraped into the pot. When they looked, where there was water a few minutes ago, now was fat moose meat. He found another bone, and when another pot was boiling, he scraped in that also. All looked closely, and in an instant, it was filled with fat bear meat. A third time he hauled a bone and scraped it into a pot and put it back, and in a twinkling of an eye, was fat beaver meat where before was water.

Kluskap dealt out this to the great combination of powers, and they had a great feast. This time Mi'kmwesu thought it would be a good plan to get Kluskap to go with them to Thunder Island to the wedding. Mi'-kmwesu asked the Great Spirit if he could come. Kluskap refused to go. He said to Mi'kmwesu, "I will lend you my canoe. It is on the shore."

The Mi'kmwesu went down and returned, saying, "I can't find the canoe."

Great spirit said, "Go down again." There was a great cliff there. Kluskap turned this one over, and there was the stone canoe with stone paddles.

These great powers came down to the shore and stepped into the canoe and went to Thunder Island, where was Mr. and Mrs. Thunder, *Kaqtukwaq;* Young Thunder, *Kaqtukwasi's,* and Miss Thunder. When they landed on the island, the great men wanted to step out, but the two little Thunders said, "Never mind." They seized the canoe and carried the men way back on the island, where they gently stepped out onto the island.

Mi'kmwesu told the Thunder, "I have a great young man here. He is the Earthquake, and I thought he would get your daughter."

Before the marriage, the Thunder says, "We must have a dance." They had it, and as Earthquake stepped around the island, the mountains fell level with the sea. Whirlwind came, and Heat Lightning destroyed the sky over them.

At this time, Kluskap was on the island. He says, "You would destroy what I'm master over." He said to the Whirlwind, "You go and travel over the world." He said the same to Heat Lightning and Thunder. "Mi'kmwesu, you go into the world and make wars with the people."

These men were people, and here they are. Heat Lighting is in the sky.

Thunder is in the sky. Whirlwind is in the sky. And Mi'kmwesu is making war between all the great tribes of North America. If they had not believed Mi'kmwesu, they all would be Indians yet. Young Earthquake never returned. He is making destruction in the bowels of the earth.

South and North

All corners of the globe — South, West, North, and East — were all human once. This is about when them directions were all human and disobliged Kluskap in a way. They were put in this world as Indians to do as he told them to.

This is about the Princess of the South. She possessed all the atmosphere of the South. Her grandmother used to come to see her. The Princess was kind of solitary and would rather live alone and not see anyone. Only her grandmother used to come. Her grandmother was the Mist, the warm rain. Warm showers to sprinkle nature's flowers that grew round her surroundings, round her camp, the wigwam, and also to sprinkle the boughs. The Princess would pick boughs, for bedding or floor of the wigwam, and her grandmother would sprinkle them and make them green and fresh.

Finally, one day when her grandmother wasn't present, the Princess was gazing over those hills north. As she looked away north, she discovered beautiful mountains glittering. Silver and gold they appeared, like a beautiful moss of silver and gold. One of the mountains was the Princess's grandfather, and when the sun rose from the east and glittered those very mountains, they appeared to her as gold and silver.

Then her grandmother appeared to her, and she told her grandmother, "Oh, I saw beautiful mountains away north, and they shone gold and silver to me. I would like to go there."

Her grandmother says to her, "Oh, that's your grandfather. You must not go there. You can't live with him. I lived with him as long as I could until I came where you are, to get peace." Her grandmother came and sprinkled those beautiful boughs. Then she went away again.

While she was away, the Princess went to see those beautiful silver mountains. She had long black hair, and the further north she went, it snowed on her hair and turned it the colour of the snow, white. She approached to what she thought was this beautiful mountain, and she found out that it was her grandfather, as her grandmother told her of. And he abused her.

When she was missing, her grandmother told the people of the South and the people between the South and West and the people between the South and East and the people of the East, also the people of the West, to get up all the warriors from all those points and war against the North, the Princess's grandfather. They fought a desperate battle before they could get the Princess back, and they brought her back after this desperate battle. But she never was as she was before she went.

When the Princess returned after her trouble going to her grandfather, she died a little while afterwards, after they got her back. And in her dying bed, she told those who were around about her, "You will remember me, and there'll be signs unto the end of the world. You will remember my words when it will be raining and when it will be hailing and when it will be snow flurries. Some hail like rain and some like ice. And blustery. And be big fall of snow and be great ice crust in the winter. This will occur every year, and you can remember I have told you these things."

Then Kluskap came, and still they were at war with one another, the South and the North. When he came, he said, "All you who are in this war, you will turn to these things." They went against Kluskap, and he punished them by turning them to hail, snow, ice crust, deep snow, and thaw. These were all human at first, and Kluskap then turned them into what they are today. Kluskap came for this purpose.

Mi'kmaw display at the Eleventh Annual Geological Congress, Oldham, 1913. Elizabeth Paul and Jerry Lonecloud are standing at the centre.
(NSM, N-1662)

Kluskap's Travels

Kluskap's camp was the point at Advocate Harbour. His stationary wigwam was at Advocate Harbour. That is where he lived at the point or neck of Advocate Harbour. There was a beaver dam there from Cape Blomidon to Spencer's Island, about nine miles across. Kluskap being a great hunter, he wanted to kill one of these beavers for his food. He set a deadfall, set a trap on Blomidon. A trap made of wood. Deadfall is a wooden trap.

When Kluskap had a deadfall on Blomidon side, he drove stakes for the beaver. Cape Split is Kluskap's trap for the beaver. The two cliffs are two stakes which were driven down into the ground when he made a deadfall for the beaver. So that if the beaver came up or down, he would get into the deadfall.

The stakes turned to stone and have been there ever since. They are known as Cape Split. The third stick fell in many years ago. The one stick is still there, and the other is the mainland or promontory of Cape Split. These three made the deadfall. The third was north of the second. The first was Cape Split. The second rock can't be climbed. It is round and smooth. Tide and ice took the third rock away. Newell Jeddore told me he remembered when the third rock was standing. When he was a boy, he used to get gull eggs from the nests of the gulls in the crannies.

This is the legend of Cape Split. After Kluskap built the deadfall at Blomidon, he did not catch any beavers. They wouldn't go in the trap. So he took his bow and stuck it above the upper part of that beaver dam. With that he slewed the beaver dam out of business. So his plan was to kill one of the beavers as the water was leaving Truro Bay or Basin, whatever it is called.

You want to know how we call Truro? *We'kopekitk,* "as far as it flows." That's where you get Cobequid. *Kopitek* is the Indian name for Berwick. Means "beaver slide." The beavers riled the waters up in Truro Basin, made it muddy-looking, so the beavers escaped unseen by him. This is why Truro Bay is so muddy. The beavers went out in the Bay of Fundy.

Then Kluskap went to Saint John to the falls there. He thought the beavers would go up the St. John River, and he would head them off. They didn't go up there. He looked at the Brier Island. It was a point at that time. He saw a beaver going over the neck of land. He picked up a stone, fired it at the beaver, and missed it. Forty miles away it was. And made a channel. The stone cut the neck of land and made it a little passage, called Petite Passage now.

The other beavers — there were two, he missed the first — went on the western part of the island, and at Brier Island Passage, they made a passage. It is there now. That island is the stone Kluscap threw. It is a little island with a lighthouse on it.

Kluskap missed both beavers and returned to his camp at Advocate. There was some beautiful stones there, amethysts. These he made beads of and wore them for good luck. Then he went to Cape Breton Island, leaped over. Here he discovered the same beavers. He killed the smallest beaver with bow and arrow and had a great feast by himself. He always lived alone. Then he was satisfied with what he had got for all his trouble. A bone found here, on Cape Breton Island, of the animals existing here before the flood, is in the museum and is supposed to be one of the bones of these beavers.[3]

Then Kluskap went back to Advocate to his old camp again. Where he got his water to drink was at Parrsboro, fifteen miles from camp, from a lake called Kluskap Lake. When he came back, he told the people and told his dogs — he had two dogs — he was going away north.

"I will come back at the end of the world. I am going to make you a happy hunting ground."

He says to his dogs, "Now we will have a moose chase." They chased the moose. They calculated to kill the moose but didn't, and the dogs chased him in the water of Advocate Harbour. The moose was swimming out toward Isle Haute or Spencers Island, and when Kluskap came to the shore, he says to the moose, "I am going to leave you here for a landmark. You turn to stone, moose." And until twenty years ago, there was a stone island, a perfect shape of a moose. But twenty years ago, the head of the moose disappeared owing to storms.

Kluskap went back to his camp without any moose, and he went up to get some water out of Kluskap Lake. He saw a partridge when he was getting the water. He didn't have his bow and arrow, and he took a stick and chased the partridge to the shore of Truro Basin or Cobequid Bay, Partridge Island. The partridge waded out into the water. Kluskap couldn't reach it to hit it with the stick he had. "Now," he says to the partridge, "now I'm going to leave you for a landmark. You will be an island, and your feathers will turn to trees." They call it Partridge Island in Parrsboro.

Then Kluskap went back to his wigwam at Advocate Harbour. Kluskap's camp was at the Head, west of the copper mine, at the end of the point. After he had some dried meat, he told his people and his dogs, "Now I am going away to leave you." Then he went north, and at Memramcook, he leaped across Memramcook to the west side. And then at the Seven Sisters, from Advocate to Memramcook. The rocks are called Seven Sisters. When he leaped from Memramcook to West Memramcook,

Klakopn,
apparently white hellebore;
its leaves look rather like
corn, and it is poisonous.
Silas Rand's *Micmac-
English Dictionary* gives
the following definition:
"*alkoose*: a poisonous
plant growing like corn;
White Hellebore (named
by Dr. Dawson from
Dr. Rand's description)."

the two dogs went as far as the Head of Advocate. All landmarks that Kluskap left.

Then Kluskap leaped from Memramcook to West Memramcook, to somewhere where Albert Mines are. He looked back from West Memramcook and saw his dogs on the Head of Advocate Harbour. Advocate Harbour has Heads, Southern and Northern Heads. The dogs were on the Northern Head, howling for their master. Kluskap lifted his hand and said, "Stay there until I come back." And they were turned to stone. These can still be seen on this Northern Head of Advocate.

At Advocate, you can see Kluskap's Medicine Garden. *Klakopn* is the name of a plant growing as tall as corn and having the same appearance as corn. Only no ears. It is poison and can be handled only by Indians. It was used by Kluskap. Kluskap was a doctor or a medicine man, and he grew his medicine in his garden. Kluskap was great with all things, but a great medicine man.

Advocate Harbour. Kluskap's residence is at Advocate Cape, where the copper mine is, at the outer end. Must go at high tide by water, from Advocate. Kluskap's camp is a rock on Advocate Point. His medicine garden is also here on the east side of his wigwam. Go on the south side of the point, look carefully, and you will see Kluskap's camp. On the east side is a sloping down towards the water on the south side. On the east side is a flat rock, which was Kluskap's garden. In the rock can be plainly seen sticks to hold the birch barks together to make back part of the camp. Withies or slats sewn between the birch bark to make a sheet for back part of camp. All is seen in rock.

Kluskap's three nieces and his grandfather. These nieces, all sisters, were the last three who attempted to accompany Kluskap when he took his bow and leapt across nine miles to Cape Wolf. Albert Mines below Hillsboro in New Brunswick. Kluskap went north. They were crying, and he said, "You also turn to stone and be known as the Three Sisters."

Kluskap's grandfather heard of these things. He spoke to the images, but there was no reply. He then waded out into the water from Advocate Head, and when he stepped into the channel, he fell in and became a reef of rock. He is called Kulpujot, which means, "you must pry him up." This ended him, and Kluskap went on.

Scraps of moose tallow, caribou tallow, bear fat, seal fat, and porpoise fat — these were a favorite lunch or choice food of Kluskap's. They were provided by the Wikulatmu'jk. Kluskap stayed in Cape Breton, and the Wikulatmu'jk came to Cape Breton, where the Beefsteak Rock is. When they came to Cape Breton, the Wikulatmu'jk told him of the beef scraps, rocks at Parrsboro. Kluskap said, "Take a few." And the remainder were left there and are still to be seen. Also Kluskap's dish at Memramcook where he had a light lunch. The stone or resting place where he sat is still there. He was there on his way north.

Kluskap ate a light lunch, called a *pepkiktaqma'sit.* Left a great big stone dish at the Indian Reserve at the top of the hill, on the path for the short cut at Memramcook. The Indians also rest here when they climb the hill each way, to give it respect. No matter how hurried you are, you set down where Kluskap sat. You can get a picture of the dish and resting place there. Only one Indian family named Knockwood is left there. The woman who told me about this married Peter Gload at Shubenacadie. Said she was brought up at Memramcook. Knockwood, Indian Chief at Memramcook. Two miles from Dorchester.

Kluskap went up the St. John River to Fredericton. He camped out at where Fredericton city is located. This is the first encampment he made after leaving his own camp at Advocate. Here he saw a beaver going down the river. He had gone quite a distance a few miles away, and Kluskap struck him with a stone. He killed the beaver, and the same stone is still in the middle of the river, the only stone there. Then Kluskap had a great feast with the beaver, and called all his tribe together to have the last meal.

In Kluskap's wigwam the "sticks" are fossilized plants, still seen today in the rocks of that locality.

Knockwood, originally *Nokut* (meaning now lost), a Mi'kmaw personal name in use as a surname as early as 1708.

He told them he was going north to make a new hunting ground.

One asked him, "What you making this new hunting ground for?"

Kluskap said, "This hunting ground shall be taken away from you by white people, but I am going north to make this new hunting ground where no white people will enter. When these white people come, you'll give them the land." That is why, when the white people came, the Indians made no disturbance and gave everyone what they wanted of the land.

He told them, "No one can come where I'll go, but I'll come again." Then he departed from there, and his next camping ground was at Gaspé on the Bay of Chaleur. It was called Gaspé because it was a landmark of Kluskap when he stopped there. He stopped there and hunted there. This time he was after caribou, and this time he was lucky and killed a caribou with his bow and arrow.

He called the people here together — they were people ahead of him — to have this great feast off this caribou. This time there were so many gathered around him, the people thought, "How is this one caribou going to feed so many?" He told one of the young men to put on two big pots, made of clay and grass. They had some meat roasted and some cooking, and Kluskap served those meats to all. After he took out the meat, they looked at the pots again, and they were all refilled by some great miracle. He took some more out and served them. They looked back the second time, and there was just as much meat in the pots.

He served them all in this great feast with this one caribou, and they had a good deal left for anyone who came along. His people desired to go on his journey north where he was going to prepare this new hunting ground. He says, "No one can come with me. You can't come." And he started off again.

Next stop Kluskap made was further north. And his next camping place was at the mouth of St. Francis River, forty-one miles below Montreal, where the St. Francis River runs into the St. Lawrence. Panu'k River is Indian name for St. Francis. He stayed the next while here. Those people he gave a great feast to desired to go with him. They tracked him as far as they could but were overtaken with snow and ice and had to return home. One great man said, "We try it again." But they failed again.

Kluskap's next camping ground was away north, and this was the last place. It was a curious thing that happened here. Kluskap gave the last feast. He said there would be no more. It was a feast of sturgeon, and there was meat in the fish. This was the miracle. They gathered here again, and this was the last feast. It was north before you come to Labrador, although Labrador was not known then.

Kji-kien, possibly "the great one." *Meltamiwej,* possibly "the first one." *Ksu'skw,* hemlock; *Nimnoqinuk,* yellow birch; *Qasqusi,* cedar.

Howsomever, this was the last feast to be given, and there would be no more. He killed a sturgeon in the river with bow and arrow. He told them, "You can't go where I'm going." He told them of coming again and bade them goodbye. "You'll see me no more until I come again."

The Indian Warriors were *Kji-kien* and *Meltamiwej.* These are the greatest of all warriors in the world in their time. These are graded down to three more, not so great: *Ksu'skw, Nimnoqinuk,* and *Qasqusi.* After Kluskap went north, Kji-kien said to Meltamiwej, "Let's go to Kluskap's." Kluskap had said, "No one can come to me, but I'll come again at the last day." These warriors were great witches. So they got a band of warriors commencing from *Kespukwitk,* Yarmouth, "end of land."

Kji-kien started from Kespukwitk through Shelburne to Halifax and Cape Breton. Meltamiwej went along the Bay of Fundy up the St. John River with his band of warriors. And thirty-four miles over to Rivière du Loup and the St. Lawrence, to meet at the mouth of the St. Francis River. They met at the St. Francis River. All started for the north, where Kluskap was.

They met with great difficulty with other tribes and had war. With every tribe they met, they were outnumbered. The last place they were was in Labrador among the Mountaineers or Seacoast Indians of the north. Here they got into a big encampment.

There was great witchcraft among the Mountaineers, and they set up a long pole. There was a young pup of a wolf here. Kji-kien and Meltamiwej were told, "If any of you can go up the pole and bring down the young wolf, then you can go further north." Kji-kien said he would go up and take the pup down. He climbed and brought the pup down in his cap.

So the Great Chief of the Mountaineers said, "You people can go on with no further trouble. You have overpowered us."

Many of his warriors returned home, what had not been killed off by the wars before. But Kji-kien, Meltamiwej, Ksu'skw, Nimnoqinuk, and Qasqusi — the five greatest warriors — went on to see Kluskap. This is the last time Kluskap was seen by the Mi'kmaq. These five got there to Kluskap's. When they got to Kluskap's wigwam, Kluskap asked them what they wanted, coming all the way here.

Ksu'skw had first choice. What he wanted, what he desired. He said he wanted a long life. "I want to live long." Kluscap asked Nimnoqinuk what he wanted. "I want to live long," Nimnoqinuk replied. He asked Qasqusi what was his wish. He said he would wish to live to the end of the world.

Kluskap said, "All right." These were warrior men. He took Qasqusi by the hair of the head and twisted his neck. He said, "You'll live to the end of the world." He formed him into a cedar tree. You can see the bark of the cedar today is twisty. Nimnoqinuk wished to live long. Kluskap took hold of him, stood him outside his wigwam door, and formed him into a yellow birch tree. Today you see yellow birches in the Forks at the Margaree River. Where the river forks, there is a yellow birch hundreds of years old. Yellow birch is a long-lived tree. It stands out today as Kluskap stood that tree, Nimnoqinuk. Straight with many branches. The branches were feathers of the cap Nimnoqinuk wore.

Kluskap said to Ksu'skw, "Now I'm going to give you your wish." So Kluskap took Ksu'skw out of his camp and stood him alongside of Nimnoqinuk. Ksu'skw became a hemlock tree. Ksu'skw was bare-headed. He had no headdress on, and his hair was sticking out. This formed the branches and spills, hemlock spills, hanging down. The hemlock tree is also long-lived.

Kluskap turned around and asked Kji-kien, "What is your wish?"

Kji-kien said, "My wish is, Kluskap, I want to go back home." He had seen his three companions turned into trees.

Kluskap said, "I'll let you go with that. With all the trouble you put on yourself to come to see me."

Kluskap asked Meltamiwej his wish. He said, "I want to go home to my own native land." He also had seen the others turned to trees.

Kluskap said, "You can go also, and you can tell the people they'll see the signs of those three warriors. What they wished. You see them standing before you. You'll camp among them, but they'll never speak." That is why the Indians likes to camp among the trees.

Kluskap told them not to come, because he'll be coming and will show them this greater place further north. And all the Indians have been looking ever since for him to come and show them that greater place way far north.

That ended that story.

A Woman Dreams the First Canoe

Origin of the Canoe. This Indian woman's husband used to go on foot around the lakes to see his traps. And when he wanted to go on the opposite side, he always hunted up a crossing place and jumped from rock to rock until he reached the other side or walked over a fallen tree. After he crossed the river, he would go down to its mouth where it enters the lake, and if there was any game in the deadfall, he would take it out and hang it on the limb of a tree until he returned. Then he would go along around the lake until he came to another river or big brook which emptied in the same lake. If there was any game in this trap, he would do as he did with the other — hang it on the limb of a tree.

Sometimes he would see the game in the trap on the other side of the river. Then he would have to go up to a crossing place away up. Then he would take this out of the trap and hang it up at the outlet of the lake. He didn't get no game, but he saw game in the trap on the opposite side, the side he lived on. He went back and took the game he had hung on the tree. Then he went up to this crossing place and crossed there. Then he went down where his second game was.

All this time his wife saw him.

Then he took that on his back and went up to the first one he had caught at the outlet of the lake. Then he went back up where he had crossed first. He had a great burden on his back, having all those games, and his wife sympathized with him. "That's too bad you have so hard time getting those games. There's no way to avoid this. If we move over on the other

A typically shaped Mi'kmaw canoe and a wigwam, by Malti Pictou's house, Bear River, about 1900. The men are Malti Pictou, Jerry Lonecloud, and John McEwan, all noted guides. (Glass negative by Harry Cochrane or Ralph N. Harris; NSM, 97.31)

side, when you got this game, we would frighten the game to this side. Then you would be obliged to come on this side again."

The old man says to his wife, "Oh, I saw a game in the trap on the other side when I was at the last trap which had nothing in it where I turned to come back, and I'll go down to that now, on our side of the river."

The woman, she dreamed about how to manufacture a canoe, the first one ever invented. She dreamed it in succession for three nights until it was all completed.

The woman's first dream was to put birchbark for the canoe, and her second dream was to sew the bark together and to make the frame of the canoe and make a gash into the pine trees for pitch. Meantime she dreamed about the way to get the young spruce roots to sew the canoe bark with. Her third dream was to finish the canoe and have the canoe paddles made.

She did all that, and she told her husband, "Step right into the canoe."

The man doubted this could take them to the other side. He said, "I don't want to because I'll step right . . . step right down to the bottom." She persuaded him to step in, and the canoe held him up. He put both feet in, and the canoe held him up. He sot down in the bottom of the canoe. He was scared. He looked on both sides. Here he was on top of the water.

She stepped in aft and paddled him acrost to the opposite side where the river went in the lake. All this time he didn't dip his paddle. He was so amazed to see how this could take him over to where he had his deadfalls. When they landed on the other side, they found two beavers, one in each trap on the opposite side.

She told him (she had to tell him everything), "You step out, and I'll hold the canoe. Open the trap, take the beaver out of the deadfall, and set the trap over again. Bring the beaver down to the canoe and put it in the canoe in the middle."

Then he got in the canoe. That woman shoved the canoe off and went over on the opposite side of the river where there was another beaver in the trap. She told him to step out of the canoe again and get that beaver out of the deadfall. And she told him to put it in the middle of the canoe again and step in.

"I'll take you up to the head of the lake where the other river came in and where your other trap is." And there was another beaver in that one. She told him, "Now you get that beaver and bring the beaver down and put it with the others in the middle of the canoe."

He got in again after that, and she shoved it off from the shore. He was at the head of the canoe. She told him to make use of the paddle. He was ahead, and she was aft. "What am I to do?" he said.

She said, "Look back, see me paddle the water to make the canoe go, and by your help, we'll make it go faster, so we'll get home soon." And he did so, and by that they went twice as fast as they did when she paddled alone. They got to their camping ground, and there weren't one pound of beaver meat on his back where he used to have the whole heft on. The man and woman took the beavers out of the canoe.

The man got interested in the canoe. He did not know what to make of it at first. He said, "What are we going to do to this canoe?"

She said, "Take the bow and lift it out of the water, and I'll take the stern and lift it out of the water, and we carry it into the woods to our camp. Now we can move it any time, anywheres you want to, around the points, around this lake, whenever you want to, wherever you like. We can shoot the rapids easy enough, but coming back, we'll have to rise a pole for to go upstream with."

There are points in the lake, and they went across to a point and camped there. Here they could look back on where the canoe was built on their old camping ground. They went to another point of the lake and could see the latter point. They left, but not from that point where the canoe was built. Then they poled the canoe upstream. They did not go downstream first. They tried the hardest thing first. And they came to falls and could go no further. They stopped at the foot of the falls.

The woman said to her man, "What is it like up above?" Because he had been used to travelling so much. He told her, "There is a long deadwater up above here, but we can't go no further than here."

Then they left the canoe at the foot of the falls. She says to him, "Show me this deadwater, how far is it and where." They started off together. They hadn't gone far before they came to the deadwater. She says, "Now we'll go back to the canoe." When they got back there, she says to him, "You take that canoe on your back and the paddles, and I'll take the dunnage." So he did so, and she says to him, "You follow me, and I'll sing out. You can't see much with a canoe on your head. I'll sing out once in a while, and you come to my voice, and I'll tell you when to stop."

They got to the foot of the fall. This would make it portaging. This is the first name that was introduced of carrying place or portage. They put the stuff in the canoe and went up this beautiful deadwater. Lots of animals there all around them. Deadwater is a wide stream but no run to it until you get to the head of the deadwater where you get falls again. Deadwater is not a lake. It is wider than a river. Animals come down to drink. At the head of this deadwater were very wild rapids, and they could not pole the canoe up. They were obliged to lug the canoe again into a lake.

First of all, she asked what was above there and he told her, as he was all the time in the woods, "A beautiful lake and islands in the lake." She liked the sound of that, the islands. Where she was brought up, there were no islands in that lake, and she would like to see that. Whatever they were

— islands. And she said, "You'll have to lug the canoe up to the lake."

Well, they go into the lake and into the canoe. She liked the scenery very well. Now he told her of an island, although he had never been on the lake. He took his paddle and pointed out to a piece of land and said, "That is an island. I have walked all around this lake and still the land is there in the lake, so it must be an island." He said, "Now we'll land in some part of that land in the lake."

They selected out a beautiful cove in the lake into the island, and she heard all kinds of birds, wild birds, there. She said, "These birds, that's where they hatch their young." She was a great lover of birds. She told her husband, "This is the place we're going to live till I die." And she ended her time on the bird island in the lake. The birds loved her, and she used to talk to them.

Amasiku and the Feast That Never Was

Amasiku had children, and one of the boys got married. They had a great wedding feast with of all kinds of birds and animal flesh, and had great dances. Amasiku was advised to have a dance also. He said he would, and he took his time about it. His son and his wife went away after the great dance, and so did all the rest who were in the wedding feast. Finally, when they were all gone, Amasiku took to dancing alone. He made a circle dancing around until he wore the ground down. He danced continuously for a year, until next time. They always met there every year, and he danced until some of his people came there and caught sight of him now and then as he bobbed up and down it.

"What are you doing here?" they said.

"I'm dancing to my son's wedding," he said. "If you say stop, it'll be all right."

He left them all there to go through whatever ceremonies they had to do, and he went into the forests. He came across a screech owl. It was setting on a tree, and it looked at Amasiku, and Amasiku looked at the owl. Amasiku began to turn around and took his time, took his time, took his time, all the while the owl looking at him, the owl continuing to twist his head until his head came off and dropped on the ground. Amasiku picked the head up and took it to the encampment. He says, "Here's a bird here I brought. He looked strange at me until he looked his head off. We must have great feast on this. I'll be the head of it."

And then his children would come up to him and say, "What time are you going to have this great feast?"

"Oh well, sometime."

Then another one would come up, and also his relatives, to ask what time the feast was going to be. "Oh, I'll be ready soon." But this soon never came. His old friends also came and wanted to know, and he put them off that way until time was over. They used to go from south to north for powwow to meet Kluskap. The last one came, and he said, "Oh, it'll be on sometime." And that's all you could get out of him. So they all went and left him. He was there the next year with the owl's head yet, and then they expected to have that great feast this next year. But still he said, "Oh, I will let you know."

One of Amasiku's younger children said, "Father, I saw a moose track coming here." He asked the child where, and he was told and it was showed to him. Now he took a piece of stick, a little twig, and measured the track of the moose every which way — length, width, peak of the toe part of the hoof — and said to the child, "You go back, and I'll sit here until this moose comes back and kill it for the feast."

Every moose that came along, he measured their track, but it was not the right one, the same one. Therefore he would not kill it. When it was time to meet Kluskap again, he was sitting there yet to see if the moose with the track would come. Next year when they returned, the old woman said to the child, "If you see any track at all, don't tell your father of it, for it takes him so long to get a moose."

Amasiku sat there for years. When they asked him when the feast was going to be, he would say, "When I kill this moose that has this track. Here it is."

When the children came for the next powwow, they saw a seal by the shore, and one of his children said to his father, "Oh, we saw a seal," although he had been cautioned to tell him nothing, for it took him so

Jerry Lonecloud in Truro at old Chief Peter Wilmot's hundred-and-first birthday party, 26 July 1927. Chief Wilmot is at the right. Lonecloud is at the left, holding a rifle with a bayonet and the skull and antlers of the moose shot by Wilmot when he was in his eighties. (NSARM, N-10,643)

long. Then he got his child to show him where he saw the seal. Then he launched his canoe and took his bow and arrow and went out where the seal was. But the seal dove before he could shoot him. He chased it, but every time this seal would come up, he would get his bow and arrow ready, but the seal would dive.

This went on night and day until Amasiku starved the seal, and when he floated on top of the water, he drug him in his canoe and went ashore with him and drug him on mainland, made his fire smoke. He made a fire up to the windward, and the fire blew right down to where the seal was. Seal has very keen scent. Amasiku said, "You are a great animal to scent. You can scent everybody and scent a smoke." If to leeward of him, he don't catch scent of you. "Here's your chance."

The seal was dead, so this was good sarcasm.

He left this seal on the shore near the fire, and he went to where they held the powwow to meet Kluskap. They make all this ready to have this great dance for the Great Spirit Kluskap, and they got through with Kluskap's ceremony. And before they were going away, he was asked what time they were going to have that owl feast.

"It'll be when I kill that moose that I have the measurement of the track. I have a seal that will come afterwards."

Always when asked about the feast, he said, "When I get the moose." But he was so slow. He stopped and caught the seal, but went back to the moose.

Mysterious Voices

Kewasu'nukwej, Tree-Feller, the Strong Hitter, he can fell any size tree with one blow. No one ever saw him, but you hear him in the daytime on a calm day, or at night. I heard him and went up and actually there they were, broken off, big trees. I heard him at Noel. I heard one whack alongside the road. I went in. It was a calm morning.

They think it is some great spirit, great power spirit. No one ever saw him. He'll sometimes hit a tree in the night, and it'll fall on the camps and kill and destroy what smoked meat they have for the winter. You hear him first and go out to see if you can see him. Then he stops and goes further off, and you can barely hear him in the distance. And they think they have driven him away. He'll keep doing this for generations, and still he has never been seen.

I heard the Hitter in the woods at Kejimkujik.[4] I also heard the *Se'skwej* and the Screechers in the sky at Kejimkujik. This young squaw heard the voice of the Screechers in the west, and she leapt from one rock to another, a distance no one could leap under ordinary circumstances. That's the story. Voices of Screechers travel towards the sun. Heard in the air.

At Mill Village, ask for Mr. Primrose Smith, an old man. He has the book about the Screechers, Se'skwej, voices in the sky, voices haunting in the sky. You can hear them talking and singing. The author of this book was some kind of a spiritualist. She got the story from Joe Glode at Great Lake.

A Tale About Mi'kmwesu

An Indian and his wife, a good, pious, honest man who had no name as I know of, brought up their four children, two girls and two boys. They thought the world of them. The boys did not live with their parents. They did not dwell in one room. There were two departments in the camp. The young men had their doorways away from the others. The others didn't allow the boys to walk past before them.

The old man used to go hunting and trapping, generally starting out in the summer and staying until the fall. Then come down with the bales of pressed meats of different kinds for their winter supplies. He kept this up until he died.

Then the oldest boy went away. They didn't know where he went to. The youngest boy was staying home, and the food was about run out. He says to his mother, "I'll go and take my father's canoe and go up the river the way he used to go to get game." He went up where he had never gone with his father until he found a landing place where his father used to land. He followed the trail until he came to the camp where his father used to camp. He stayed there all night. Next day he started out setting deadfalls for bears, beavers, and otters. He was away all day, and at evening he came to that camp.

As he opened the wigwam door, he saw a woman setting down in the wigwam. He was much surprised to see that. He had never seen a woman, only his mother. She said, "Oh, I'm so glad to see you, I was expecting you since your father died to come and trap up here, as I used to keep camp for him." She had everything ready cooked for him and wood gathered for him for the night. He was much surprised. He didn't know what to do. He thought 'twas Mi'kmwesu. Which she was.

There is a Mi'kmwesu man and a Mi'kmwesu woman. He thought

Mi'kmwesui'skw, the female manifestation of a Mi'kmwesu.

Keskiju'naqien, "to jump over."

Mi'kmwesue'jit — that is the old man's name — was after him. That he had changed himself to Mi'kmwesui'skw. Mi'kmwesu was her name. He thought that because she was so pretty, and her dress was ornamented with teeth of animals. Her headdress was a peaked cap, ornamented with feathers of different birds. Mi'kmwesu is the evil one who can change himself to different forms. If he is after a man, he can form himself into an Indian woman. Mi'kmwesu forms any way. The boy thought this was Mi'kmwesu.

She said, "This is the way I used to have everything ready for your father."

The boy stayed all night. In the morning bright and early, he shoved his canoe across on the other side of the river. He started north. Then he came up on a high hill. He looked down on the valley and saw smoke and wigwams, encampment as he thought. He was a stranger altogether. He thought he would go down to that encampment.

At the first camp he came to was an old woman. Her name was *Nem-oogeeistchquitch,** or "great witch." This was the second woman he had met. He had been brought up virtuous and righteous and knew nothing of the outside world. His brother had gone into the world and married, but he did not know this.

When the young man came up to the camp, she called him in. She said, "I wanted to see you long ago. The place where you stayed last night was Mi'kmwesu. He is a very bad man, and I'm glad you left there. Don't you go back there any more." She guessed his thoughts. "When you saw her, you wished you hadn't gone there and wanted to get away, and you're away now and can stay with me for a while."

"There is going to be great ball playing in this *utank,* the centre of this encampment." *Tu'aqn,* or ball playing. Last game was played sixty years ago at Digby. "Scaling the tops of wigwams, *keskiju'naqien* during the game. And I want you to be into the game." She had no children, and she put all her wish with him to win the game and so on.

"I'll tell you when the time is appointed, so you can be in the game.

And you'll gain the game, and you'll bring the tu'aqn, the ball made of stone, to me."

He did. He scaled the wigwam and caught the ball on the last heat. They had six plays. The game is played with a stone ball. The chief throws the ball in the air, and some of the young men jump to catch it before it reaches the ground and scale the first wigwam they come to, the others chasing after them. After one of them scales the wigwam and holds the ball, he takes it back to the chief. This was done six times on this occasion. The one who takes it most times to the chief has the game and is entitled to the chief medicine man's daughter. The young man got all six and took the ball to the great witch woman.

She says, "That ball is yours now, but they'll try and get it from you."

They were all frightened of her. She was a great witch woman. He stopped there. She said, "Now you can keep this ball. There is going to be a great war in another encampment between two tribes, and your brother will be in the war, and he'll be killed. This ball will be a weapon of yours, and whatever you want it to do, it will do. You can throw it, and it will kill. But it will be too late by the time you get to the war. Your brother will be killed in the battle, but you'll see him."

He started on according to the witch woman's directions. She said, "Your brother is living beside one of the biggest wigwams there, but there'll be enemies and they'll be scattered all through the woods." He started, and the war was on when he got there. When he got to his brother's wigwam, his brother had gone into the war. He took the stone ball and used it as a weapon for to kill off the enemies. He saw his brother during the struggle, but his brother fell. The enemies shot him with arrows.

Then he got raging, and he killed off all the rest of the Indians with the stone ball the witch told him to use. After the war was over, he went to his brother's home, and he told his brother's wife that her husband was killed. They brought him home, made a scaffold, put him on top the scaffold, and smoked him so he could be buried in a year's time. He took the ball that he won the battle with home to his mother. When he got there, he says to her, "My brother was killed in the war, and he'll be preserved till next year so we'll go to the burial."

Then two little girls, his sisters, were playing in a different part of the wigwam. They were washing their clothes. They were hanging them up to dry on a line of sunbeams which pierced through a knot hole in the wigwam. They were doing this while their brother was away. The mother showed her son where they were hanging the clothes to dry. He peeked in and the clothes dropped off the sunbeams. Then he says to his mother, "My father, he was Mi'kmwesue'jit. But we must now all live together as long as we can and lead a good life for the rest of our lives." Which they did, and that ended that.

Wikulatmu'jk: The First Ones Here

The last and yet the first. The fairies were the first Indians here. The Indian name for fairies is *Wikulatmu'jk,* small people, midgets. They were the first Indians here, and they lived upon hunting fowl, all kinds of wild fowl. There were no animals at that time. The Mi'kmaq and Maliseet came and discovered them here, and it seems they understood one another. Had the same language.

The Mi'kmaq said, "Yes, we would like to stay with you, and we could live together in this way. I have the animals, and you have the birds. And if I want a bird, I'll swap him for my animal meat."

So they both agreed, and the agreement was drawn up on the rocks on Fairy Lake at Kejimkujik on the terms named. And some of the pictographs on Fairy Lake are these agreements, and what will happen to the Mi'kmaq, and signatures. But no living Indian can read them today. Agreements that they would live together, and that one would have the birds and the other, the animals. And they would exchange when they wished and not to marry between. The Mi'kmaq not to marry the Wikulatmu'jk, and the Wikulatmu'jk not to marry the Mi'kmaq.

But the Wikulatmu'jk said, "We're going to leave you because there are going to be white people here, and they will take the hunting ground from you. But we won't be here."

Wikulatmu'jk marks are on fairy rocks. Some of the birds are very large, ten or fifteen feet tall, and some of the feathers are seen in head-dresses. And serpents are pictured by the Indians. They were also in the world at the time. The Wikulatmu'jk Indian said, "I was here first and I'll be the last. You'll always see my signs on the rocks."

This legend has been lost since the first discovery of North America by the white race. This story goes back to the times before the flood. The Wikulatmu'jk were people of their word. Not one of them were left, although traces of them are found in their caves and also places in North America.

In the western states of America, the Wikulatmu'jk were great corn raisers and lived only on vegetables, life vegetation, and fruit. We still have their name, Indian Corn. The Indian Wikulatmu'jk were stronger than the big Indians. They also had witchcraft. They were great lovers of canoes and travelled around the waters. That is why they were so fond of Nova Scotia. So many lakes and streams. In Nova Scotia, they lived on fowls, clams, and lobsters.

The principal place traces of the Wikulatmu'jk are found is at Kejimkujik. Birds, spirits, and serpents were drawn by them at Kejimkujik. Traces are also found at Port L'Hebert next to Port Mouton; Liscomb; Spanish Ship Bay at Gaspereau Brook, Big Liscomb; Dutch Settlement; and another at Crow's Nest, Melrose, Guysborough County. At Melrose, there was a fairy cave at the Crow's Nest, but it has been destroyed because gold was found in the cave, and the cave was extended. At Dutch Settlement, there is a large cave on the Shubenacadie River. You can enter this cave from the bank when the water is low.

Spanish Ship Bay at Gaspereau Brook, Big Liscomb. Just before you come to the iron bridge, there is a house down at the mouth of the brook. About three hundred yards from there, on the west side of the brook, are the marks on the rocks of the Wikulatmu'jk. You have to go in a boat. There is a house opposite. The marks are on a rock, written as one would write on a wall, not flat rocks, as at Kejimkujik. They must have been done from a canoe. Foreign sailors later put their marks on the rock. The marks are still very plain. The woman in the house, a widow, would know. She had some Indian relics, Indian arrows and spearheads when she dug up her ground.

At Port L'Hebert, next to Port Mouton, near Barrington, on Post Road after leaving Port Mouton, and just before coming to Port L'Hebert, there is a good-sized brook. The cave is this way from Port L'Hebert, right near the bridge. There is a big cliff and a hole there. There is a mill there now. Across the bridge, there is a stone where the fairies manufactured their arrowheads, where chips are still to be seen.

Across from the cave, a hundred yards, is a bed of clam shells all neatly laid together by hundreds. Dig two feet down, and there they are, one foot deep, all so neatly piled. The brook is very near the salt water. The cave is the smallest of them all, although you can just stand up in it. You can throw a stone down it, and after a while it will strike water.

At Cape Blomidon is a big cave, about the biggest I know of. It runs in for about half a mile. The cave has a pond. It is loaded with bats. This is the furtherest the Indians went. The cave is nicely worked and smooth. Almost polished, the walls. You go to Scott's Bay, get a boat past Cape Split, about half a mile further on the Windsor side. The cave is half a mile long, and there is a pond at the end. That is as far as you can go. It is said that no one ever went across the pond. The Indians were too superstitious.

At Advocate Point, there is also said to be a fairy cave. Years ago it was occupied by the Scotch, who anchored their vessels in Advocate Harbour. They discovered copper in the cave and made pennies out of this native copper. In the summer they got it. And took it home in the winter.

In Cape Breton, there are many more caves. Fairies were also near Five Islands, four or five miles from Five Islands.

At the time of the flood, these Indian fairies disappeared. Fairy Indians. They got instruction from Kluskap that they wouldn't come under the white people here. The big people would. "You will disappear."

The flood destroyed them. I don't know for why. The Wikulatmu'jk didn't get on the iceberg. They said they would stay. They wanted to keep their word. They said, "You go." They thought the Indians were going to a different world, and they said, "We will stay here. The white man will take your land." All the rest of the noble race of Indians were destroyed by the flood.

Rock carvings at Kejimkujik, Nova Scotia. George Creed traced them. He made one set for a London museum, one for Washington D.C. One for the Halifax museum. George Creed traced over three hundred pictographs from the rocks at Kejimkujik. Drawn pictographs that no one living understands. Said to be work of the Wikulatmu'jk. That agreement between the Wikulatmu'jk and the Mi'kmaq before the flood. Two Indian women were drawn by the Wikulatmu'jk.

Later the Mi'kmaq drew things also. Prophecies of what would happen to the Mi'kmaq. They drew the world, which they thought was flat. The heaven hunting ground and Kji-kinap, creator of world and all things. And then Kinap, a mighty worker who helped to finish the world with Kluskap. Although Kluskap is not there as far as we know. The world and heaven, Kji-kinap and Kinap. The four greatest things.

At Kejimkujik, you can see petroglyphs for heaven and earth. This star is heaven.

And this triangle represents Kinap. Greater than Kluskap.

 [This] represents Kluskap.

This circle in a circle represents earth. The outside ring finishes the earth and represents vapour. Earth was thought to be flat. The inside ring represents the flat earth. The outside ring represents the water or the tumbling-off place, *Kespumk*. Indian word for "end" or "the water." The tumbling-off place, where, if you get there, you're gone.

Indians never went out of sight of land in their canoes. Off Yarmouth, there is an island called Green Island, which was supposed to be another land. One day, some Indians went in a canoe to the island and were never seen again. It was thought by the rest of the tribe that the evil spirit enticed them, and they fell over the tumbling-off place.

We never came from anywhere. We have been here since the creation. One theory is that we came from Asia, India or China along Bering Strait. Japanese say we are the lost tribe. But we are not. We are people of our own.

Kespi-a'tuksi.

Kespi-a'tuksi means, this is my last word.

ENDNOTES

ONE: *The Life of Jerry Lonecloud*

1. Arrell M. Gibson, "Medicine Show," *The American West: Magazine of the Western History Association,* 4:1 (February 1967), 35, 76, 77.

2. Clary Croft, executor for the estate of Dr. Helen Creighton, to Ruth Whitehead, 1 March 1993. Nova Scotia Museum, History Section, Mi'kmaw Heritage Resource Files, Correspondence.

3. Père Paul Pacifique, *Le Pays des Micmacs* (Restigouche, Québec: Ste Anne de Restigouche, 1935), 289.

4. Nova Scotia Museum Accession Book III: Item 4578, Lonecloud to Piers, 3 November 1917.

5. Nova Scotia Archives and Records Management, Dennis Papers, MG1, Vol. 2867, No. 2a: 28.

6. Campbell Hardy, *Sporting Adventures in the New World*, Vol. 1 (London: Hurst and Blackett, 1855), 129-130; pencil note in Harry Piers's handwriting in the margins of the Nova Scotia Museum Library copy, pages 129-130.

7. Nova Scotia Museum Library, Piers Papers, Ethnology: Material Culture: Item 7, Lonecloud to Piers, 25 February 1918.

8. Mark Neely, *The Abraham Lincoln Encyclopedia* (New York: McGraw Hill, 1982), 73.

9. Nova Scotia Museum, History Section, Mi'kmaw Heritage Resource Files, People, Jerry Lonecloud: A.J. Boyd to J.D. McLean, 19 June 1911 (photocopy of original).

10. Nova Scotia Museum Library, Piers Papers, Ethnology: Genealogies: Item 23, Lonecloud to Piers, 8 February 1919.

11. Nova Scotia Museum Accession Book III: Item 4147, 5 May 1914. Nova Scotia Museum Library, Piers Papers, Ethnology: Botany, Medicines, Item 3; Elizabeth Paul to Piers, 6 March 1931.

12. Nova Scotia Museum Library, Piers Papers, Ethnology: Micmac Correspondence, Item 7, Lonecloud to A.J. Boyd, 4 December 1917.

13. Nova Scotia Museum, History Section, Mi'kmaw Heritage Resource Files, People, Jerry Lonecloud: Ruth Legge to Ruth Whitehead, taped interview and transcript, September 1995.

14. Walter Baker to Ruth Whitehead and Trudy Sable, personal communication, July 1994.

15. Blake Conrad to Ruth Whitehead, personal communication, April 1998, April 2002.

16. *Halifax Herald*, Halifax, NS, 17 April 1930, "Lone Cloud, Medicine Man of Micmac Indians, Succumbs in Hospital"; William C. Borrett, *Down East: Another Cargo of Tales Told Under the Old Town Clock* (Halifax: The Imperial, 1945), 44-45.

17. Nova Scotia Museum Library, Piers Papers, Ethnology: Micmac Correspondence: Item 5, Lonecloud to J.D. MacLean, 17 July 1916.

18. Nova Scotia Museum Library, Piers Papers, Ethnology: Micmac Correspondence: Item 9, Lonecloud to Secretary, DIA, 20 March 1917; Item 10, Lonecloud to Secretary, DIA, 9 April 1917; Item 12, Lonecloud to Secretary, DIA, 27 November 1917.

19. Nova Scotia Museum Library, Piers Papers, Ethnology: Genealogies: Item 62, Lonecloud to Piers, 31 December 1917.

20. Nova Scotia Museum Library, Piers Papers, Ethnology: Micmac Correspondence: Item 60, Elizabeth Paul to No. 470813 Private Abram Paul, 25th Battalion Canadians, 25 February 1918.

21. Nova Scotia Museum Library, Piers Papers, Ethnology: Politics, Item 24, Lonecloud & Piers, 1 December 1924.

22. Nova Scotia Museum Library, Piers Papers, Science: Paleontology. Harry Piers, "Mastodon Remains in Nova Scotia," unpublished essay, 10 May 1912.

23. Nova Scotia Archives and Records Management, MG 1, Vol. 1049, Piers Papers, "Daily Journal," (entry for 16 April 1930).

24. Harald Prins to Ruth Whitehead. Nova Scotia Museum, History Section, Mi'kmaw Heritage Resource Files: Correspondence.

25. Harvey Boutilier to Ruth Whitehead, personal communication, 1999.

TWO: *Here's What I Remember: The Memoir of Jerry Lonecloud*

1. While linguist Bernie Francis has been able to give the literal meaning and the modern spelling for many of the words or phrases which Dennis took down from Lonecloud, in some cases it has not been possible to do so. These unrecoverable words are marked with an asterisk, and a list may be found on pages 173-174. Mi'kmaw traditional lifeways have changed greatly since Lonecloud was born. Some of the Mi'kmaw words that he used are no longer remembered; others Dennis may have heard incorrectly. There was no standardized spelling for Mi'kmaw words until the creation in the 1970s of the Francis-Smith orthography, so in any case she was guessing at the spelling. Her spelling appears in the text and in the list.

2. *Mattamalia hé.* In Silas T. Rand, *Micmac-English Dictionary*, ed. Jeremiah S. Clark (Charlottetown: Patriot Publishing, 1902), this word appears as *matamalea*, "a bride," from the French *madame marier*. Bernie Francis has heard this cheer as *ajja malia hé.*

3. Latin names provided by Alex Wilson and Marian Munro, botanists, Nova Scotia Museum.

4. John Thomas Lane, called "Paddy" because he was Irish, sold a smallpox cure in nineteenth-century Halifax. He was not a doctor but an officer at the customs house who dressed up like a Mi'kmaw. He got his cure from the wife of Chief Francis Paul, who was said to be a Mohawk.

THREE: *Stories Without End*

1. The *wikulatmu'jk* in traditional stories are smaller persons of a different culture. They became more and more like European fairies (Lonecloud himself uses this term), especially when storytellers were translating for non-natives, as they became more acculturated over time.

2. The *Mi'kmwesu'k* traditionally were human beings who had been changed by power, usually power given to them by other Mi'kmwesu'k. In stories told before the time of Jerry Lonecloud, they were seen as helpful to humans, teaching them survival skills and music. With the coming of Catholicism, many such beings in traditional tales were demonized; thus Lonecloud calls the Mi'kmwesu'k "evil."

3. This bone was actually the femur of a mastodon, but the Mi'kmaq took it as evidence of the giant beavers of their legends. The giant beaver, *Casteroides ohioensis*, became extinct about 10,000 to 8,000 years ago, but the many stories from numerous native groups about these creatures, eight feet high and ten feet long (counting the tail), testify that people did know the giant beaver in ancient times. The mastodon bone, plowed up in Cape Breton in 1834, is now on display at the Nova Scotia Museum, Halifax.

4. Lonecloud told Clara Dennis that *Kejimkujik* meant "a long way to paddle." He told Harry Piers, however, that it was a phrase in "men's language," not used around women or children, meaning "chapped and swollen testicles." This verb phrase, according to Bernie Francis, literally means, "they are painfully felt." After paddling a long way on this lake, a man's testicles would be cold and swollen, rubbed raw.

UNKNOWN MI'KMAW VOCABULARY

Jerry Lonecloud told Clara Dennis the following Mi'kmaw words and their English definitions, but linguist Bernie Francis could not trace them in modern Mi'kmaq. Mi'kmaw lifeways have changed greatly since Lonecloud learned the language, and some of the words he used may no longer be remembered. Also, although Clara Dennis did her best to spell the words Lonecloud used (sometimes with his help), she may have heard incorrectly, and there was no standardized spelling for Mi'kmaw words until the creation of the Francis-Smith orthography in the 1970s. These otherwise-unknown words, spelled as Dennis recorded them, are marked with an asterisk in the text.

Bulloomsk	female beaver
Bullomskooitch	beaver's eldest son
Cahscalegenetch	brown sparrow
Chickéégetch	chickadee
Costimas	bags of castoreum
Deardardeoalie	king bird
Gayaydumsk	male beaver
Glowgleetch	brown thrush
Goodgeebumcheeisch	beaver's oldest daughter
Hahcheyoh	sea seal
Hawyawlkes	wood duck
Kludamen	I can stay under water a long while
Mooreeawdom	bittern
Mootcoolaysenmuek	Mi'kmaw dogs
Neektoolnetch	mackerel gull
Nemoogeeistchquitch	great witch

Njilj	my father-in-law [this term has been replaced in modern times by *Niskamij*, "my grandfather," a courtesy title]
Nomatháló͓o	brown wren
Sighignish	the name of an island
Soxcohdoo	flying squirrel
Tahdahgoo, tahgahgoo	gannet
Wayelgwask	head of the lake [*We'*, "head of"; the rest of the word is unknown.]
Wisenawk	bags of castoreum
Wissadaej	teal [probably *wisowte'j*]

INDEX